Isola Filicudi · Isola Canna

Isola Salina

Canale della Salina

Isola Lipari

Isola Stromboli & Panarea ↗

Isole Eolie

Bocche di Vulcano

Isola Vulcano

Golfo di Milazzo

A20

Stretto di Messina

A18

Messina

A3

Golfo di Patti

Tindari

A20

Monti Peloritani

Parco Regionale dei Nebrodi

THE NORTHEAST

ebrodi

Gole dell' Alcantara

Mazzarò
Taormina
Giardini-Naxos

Parco Nazionale de

3323
Monte Etna

A19

Etnaland

A19

Catania

Golfo di Catania
Foce di Simeto

Piana di Catania

Piazza Armerina

Serra Pietraliscia

Golfo di Augusta

Paradise City
Parco Acquatico

Caltagirone

Monti Iblei

Parco Archeologico della Neapolis

Siracusa
Ortygia
Porto Grande

SIRACUSA & THE SOUTHEAST

A18

Comiso

Val di Noto

Noto

Riserva Naturale Pino d'Aleppo

Ragusa

li Gela

Modica

Golfo di Noto

Riserva Naturale di Vendicari

Isola Vendicari

Isola di Capo Passero

Isola delle Correnti

TWINPACK
Sicily

ADELE EVANS

AA Publishing
If you have any comments or suggestions for this guide you can contact the editor at
travelguides@TheAA.com

How to Use
This Book

KEY TO SYMBOLS

✚ Map reference

✉ Address

☎ Telephone number

🕐 Opening/closing times

🍴 Restaurant or café

🚆 Nearest rail station

🚌 Nearest bus route

⛴ Nearest riverboat or ferry stop

♿ Facilities for visitors with disabilities

❓ Other practical information

▷ Further information

ℹ Tourist information

✋ Admission charges:
Expensive (over €6),
Moderate (€3–€6), and
Inexpensive (€3 or less)

★ Major Sight   ★ Minor Sight

👣 Walks   🚐 Drives

🎁 Shops

🎭 Entertainment and Activities

🍴 Restaurants

This guide is divided into four sections

• Essential Sicily: An introduction to the island and tips on making the most of your stay.
• Sicily by Area: We've broken the island into six areas, and recommended the best sights, shops, entertainment venues, nightlife and restaurants in each one. Suggested walks and drives help you to explore.
• Where to Stay: The best hotels, whether you're looking for luxury, budget or something in between.
• Need to Know: The info you need to make your trip run smoothly, including getting about by public transport, weather tips, emergency phone numbers and useful websites.

Navigation In the Sicily by Area chapter, we've given each area its own colour, which is also used on the locator maps throughout the book and the map on the inside front cover.

Maps The fold-out map accompanying this book is a comprehensive map of Sicily. The grid on this fold-out map is the same as the grid on the locator maps within the book. The grid references to these maps are shown with capital letters, for example A1. The grid references to the town plan are shown with lower-case letters, for example a1.

Contents

Introducing Sicily

From its great volcano and its classical monuments to its sizzling beaches and gloriously rural landscape, Sicily has plenty to attract the visitor. The island has long been a crossroads between east and west, north and south, giving it a unique character.

For sunseekers, Sicily is a land of silken sands and intense blue sea. It is a paradise for walkers, bird-watchers and lovers of the great outdoors, with acre upon acre of parkland to explore. For music fans there are splendid concerts and for drama lovers there are open-air performances with stunning classical monuments as a backdrop. For foodies there are vibrant markets selling Sicilian produce and restaurants with the freshest fish you'll ever enjoy, not to mention the delicious pastries and ice cream.

Having been invaded by the Greeks, Romans, Arabs, Normans and Spanish, it is hardly surprising that Sicilians see their island as a metaphorical football being kicked around by the Italian boot of Europe. This may have contributed to Sicily's enduring sense of isolation, but it has also endowed the Mediterranean's largest and most densely populated island with a special character that draws elements from many cultures.

The great hiccup in this explosion of cultures was the emergence in the 19th century of the Mafia. The tentacles of *La Piovra* (the octopus) spread as far as the US, Canada and Australia—along with a huge number of Sicilian emigrants. In 21st-century Sicily the exodus has been stemmed and, thanks to the 1970s anti-Mafia drive and the trials of the 1980s, the influence of the criminal groups is less evident.

Although Sicily is still one of the poorest regions of Italy, the gradual erosion of extreme poverty has encouraged Sicilians to look to a rosier future in which they value the richness of their great and ancient heritage. And they warm-heartedly and cheerfully welcome the increasing number of visitors who want to share it with them.

Facts + Figures

- Population: 5,017,212
- Area: 25,426sq km (9,814sq miles)
- Economy: mainly agricultural
- Highest point: Etna, 3,323m (10,902ft)
- Government: semi-autonomous, within the Italian Republic, with its own parliament

DISTINCT FROM ITALY

The Sicilian language bears only a passing resemblance to Italian and includes many Arab words and place names. Similarly, Sicilian food is much more colourful than in mainland Italy, and includes spices and fruits, like cinnamon and dates, and an incredible variety of sugary treats.

CELEBRATIONS

There seems to be no period when there isn't some sort of festival, ceremony or procession happening in Sicily. These usually celebrate the martyrdom of one of the island's patron saints (curiously enough, among them is St. Thomas à Becket, the murdered medieval Archbishop of Canterbury). Whatever their religious fervour (and many of them invoke a certain solemnity), the festivals certainly show the Sicilians' love of an extravagantly boisterous celebration.

DID YOU KNOW?

● Sicily has officially banned smoking in public places such as restaurants, but the rules are frequently infringed.

● The British have long had a strong affinity with Sicily. As well as various writers who have congregated here, it was British merchants who introduced the island's Marsala wine to the world.

● Strictly speaking, foreigners should register with the police within two days of arrival. This usually isn't necessary because hotels do it for you.

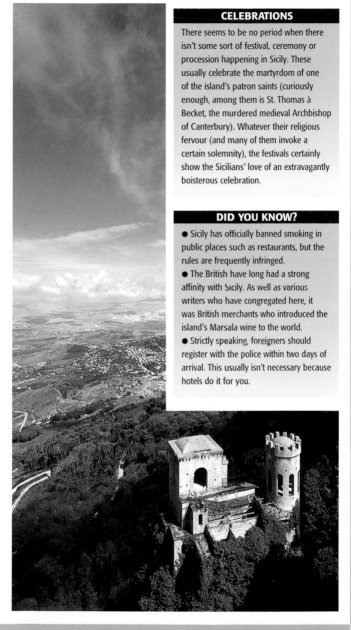

A Short Stay in Sicily

DAY 1: TAORMINA

Morning Steep yourself in history at the **Teatro Greco** (▷ 51). Arriving early, you will miss the crowds and get a good look around the site. History apart, this is arguably the best viewpoint in Sicily, encompassing the coast and southern Calabria in one direction and **Mount Etna** (▷ 49) in the other.

Mid-morning Head back along Via Teatro Greco to join Corso Umberto I, where you'll see signs for the **Giardino Público** (Villa Comunale, ▷ 50). This municipal park was created by Scottish-born Lady Florence Trevelyan. Alternatively, catch the cable car to **Mazzarò** beach (▷ 54).

Lunch From the public park take the Via Roma and rejoin Corso Umberto I by way of **Piazza IX Aprile** (▷ 50), with its restored 12th-century clocktower. You'll now be heading for the **Duomo** (▷ 50). Have a look around the piazza and the cathedral before settling down to lunch at **Al Duomo** (▷ 60).

Afternoon Take your pick of the excursions available to see **Mount Etna** (▷ 49). Apart from giving yourself a break from the heat of town in the volcano's cooler climes (yes, even though you're sitting on a volcano, it can get quite cool), it's a chance to explore the mountain's fascinating geology, flora and fauna.

Dinner There's no shortage of restaurants in the centre of Taormina, but for traditional Sicilian cuisine try **Granduca** (▷ 60), which also offers pizzas from a wood-fired oven.

Evening For an after-dinner drink head to **O'Seven** (▷ 59), where you may hear some jazz, or to any of Taormina's other lively bars.

DAY 2: PALERMO

Morning Start at Quattro Canti, Palermo's 'four corners' hub. Nearby you can find **Piazza Pretoria** (▷ 29), once called the Piazza of Shame because of its nude statues. From here take a gentle stroll westwards along Corso Vittorio Emanuele, among its many bookshops. A 15-minute walk will bring you to Palermo's magnificent Norman **cathedral** (▷ 26).

Lunch A good lunch stop is **Dietro La Cattedrale** (▷ 34), where there are outside tables, a good menu and reasonable prices.

Afternoon From the cathedral it is a short stroll northwards to the Palazzo dei Normanni and the beautiful **Cappella Palatina** (▷ 24), the Byzantine jewel in Palermo's crown. From the Piazza Indipendenza you can take bus 327 (or a longish walk) to the western fringes of Palermo and the **Convento dei Cappuccini** (▷ 25). The convent is home to the world-famous catacombs, where the remains of around 8,000 people are displayed.

Dinner Return to the city centre and make your way to Piazza Politeama (via buses 101, 102, 103, 806 or 812). Facing the **Teatro Politeama Garibaldi** (▷ 33), take the road to your right for a short distance and then turn right into Via R. Wagner to find a *ristorante tipico Siciliano*, namely **Al Cancelletto Verde** (▷ 34).

Evening From Piazza Politeama you are well-placed to find some entertainment for the evening. **Teatro Massimo** (▷ 33) is close enough, or if you're lucky you might catch a performance at the **Teatro Politeama Garibaldi** (▷ 33). Alternatively, spend the evening in one of the city's 150 discos and bars, including **I Candelai** (▷ 33), one of Palermo's hottest clubs, or the wine bar **Kursaal Kalhesa** (▷ 33).

Top 25

▶▶▶

Agrigento: Museo Nazionale Archeologico ▷ 82–83 Greek treasures and a medieval setting.

Agrigento: Valle dei Templi ▷ 84–85 A valley of sixth-century BC Greek temples.

Caltagirone: Scala di Santa Maria del Monte ▷ 64–65 A grand stairway to the past.

Taormina: Teatro Greco ▷ 51 An impressive Greek theatre, originally built in the third century BC, with Mount Etna as its backdrop.

Taormina ▷ 50 Sicily's best-loved resort offers a Greek Theatre, beautiful public gardens and some lovely sea views.

Siracusa: Ortygia ▷ 70–71 This tiny island once hosted the 'greatest Greek city'.

Selinunte ▷ 102 A fascinating Greek archaeological site strewn with temples, an acropolis and a marketplace.

Segesta ▷ 101 An unmissable hilltop Doric temple (still unfinished) and a classical theatre.

Riserva Naturale dello Zingaro ▷ 100 A magnificent coastal haven with secluded coves and beaches.

Ragusa ▷ 69 The twin towns of Ragusa Superiore and Ragusa Ibla are a mix of medieval and baroque.

Piazza Armerina: Villa Romana del Casale ▷ 86 A mosaic-rich Roman villa ruin.

Parco Archeologico della Neapolis ▷ 68 A visit to this archaeological zone is a memorable experience.

ESSENTIAL SICILY TOP 25

These pages are a quick guide to the Top 25, which are described in more detail later. Here they are listed alphabetically, and the tinted background shows which area they are in.

Cefalù ▷ 38 A small medieval harbour town with glorious swathes of sand.

Cefalù: Duomo ▷ 39 Sicily's finest Norman church, in a spectacular setting.

Erice ▷ 96 Enjoy superb views from this gem of Sicily's many picturesque villages.

Isole Eolie ▷ 48 The Aeolian Islands are isles of mystery, with tales of magical healing powers.

Marsala ▷ 97 This isolated westerly town has a history as rich as its famous wine.

Mazara del Vallo ▷ 98 A lively fishing town with a rich Moorish heritage and a sense of fun.

Monreale: Duomo ▷ 40 The Byzantine mosaics here are a narrative of Christian history.

Monte Etna ▷ 49 Explore the ever-changing landscape of Europe's liveliest volcano.

Mozia: Museo Whitaker ▷ 99 This fascinating museum lies on an island.

Noto ▷ 66–67 Sicily's finest baroque town, a 'garden of stone' grown out of the 1693 earthquake.

Isole Eolie

Cefalù

THE NORTHEAST
45–60

Taormina

Monte Etna

THE HEARTLAND &
THE SOUTH COAST
79–92

Piazza
Armerina

Caltagirone

SIRACUSA &
THE SOUTHEAST
61–78

Parco Archeologico
della Neapolis

Ortygia

Ragusa

Noto

Palermo: La Cattedrale ▷ 26–27 This magnificent cathedral was founded in the 12th century.

Palermo: Catacombe dei Cappuccini ▷ 25 A gruesome yet fascinating sight.

Palermo: Cappella Palatina ▷ 24 Palermo's greatest treasure, deep in the Palazzo dei Normanni.

ESSENTIAL SICILY TOP 25

◀ ◀ ◀

9

Out and About

Sicily is a verdant garden-cum-playground whose coastline and countryside invite exploration and offer adventure.

Water Sports
Sicily has a good choice of beaches and its many harbours are often the focus of water sports like snorkelling, scuba-diving, wind-surfing, kitesurfing, yachting and boat rides. Equipment is available for hire and there are often courses for those who want to learn—and even become expert. Beaches with good water-sports facilities include Mazzarò (▷ 54), where the snorkelling is particularly rewarding.

Walking
Hikers who like a bit of a challenge can find something to match their aspiration in a great many inland and coastal locations. Those who fancy a bit of a climb and the reward of spectacular views should head to Cefalù (▷ 38), where the vast rock La Rocca (278m/912ft) stands sentinel over the town. Sicily's other famous hiking trails are around Etna (▷ 49) and in the Parco Naturale delle Madonie (▷ 41) and the Riserva Naturale dello Zingaro (▷ 100).

Winter Sports
Sicily is probably not the first place that comes to mind when thinking of skiing, but those

---

ON TWO WHEELS

Cycling as a means of relaxation is virtually unheard of in Sicily and, given the terrain, this is understandable. Consequently, bike-hire facilities are few and far between, although cycling is becoming increasingly popular on some of the offshore islands. For the natives, cycling is strictly a sport. You'll see enthusiasts getting their bike 'fix' along quiet coastal roads first thing in the morning, but if you want to join them, you will have to bring your own wheels. In the Madonie mountains (▷ 41), the hiking notes available from tourist information offices also offer some cycling tips.

From top: Isola Bella beach, Taormina; climbing Mount Etna; beautiful scenery in the Madonie mountains

who enjoy it say there are few sensations to match tackling the lava slopes of a live volcano. Mount Etna (▷ 49) usually has good ski conditions from November to the end of March and sometimes into April. Another favourite ski spot is the tiny resort of Piano Battáglia, with its Swiss chalet-style houses, in the Madonie mountains (▷ 41, 42).

Exploring with Four Wheels

With its rugged interior, Sicily is perfect for exploration in a four-by-four vehicle. Generally, though, it's worth sticking to tried-and-tested routes. Among the best—and certainly the most spectacular for the immediate surroundings and the distant views—is the lunar landscape of Mount Etna (▷ 57).

On the Cowboy Trail

Pony trekking is widely available throughout the island. Riders can follow in the hoof-steps of the Sicilian cowboys of old, who used to herd their cattle to and from winter pasture. Check with tourist offices at Madonie (▷ 41), Nebrodi (▷ 53–54), Etna (▷ 49, 57) and Alcantara (▷ 53) for details of local treks. There's also a horse-riding school at Agrigento's Centro Ippico Concordia (▷ 91). And for passionate golfers who can't take a holiday from their favourite sport, there's an 18-hole golf course, Il Picciolo (▷ 59), in the Gole dell'Alcantara, 25km (15 miles) from Taormina.

From middle: strolling in Taormina's public gardens; a cove in the Riserva Naturale dello Zingaro

PEACE AND QUIET

Sicilian daily life isn't peaceful. Everyone seems to be busy and everyday conversations in the mellifluous Sicilian tongue sound as though they've been scored in *agitato*. But even in the high season there are places to escape to—secluded, unspoiled beaches like those at Zingaro (▷ 100). In the towns, the answer is to go native and enjoy the local *passeggiata* (evening stroll), for example in Palermo's Quattro Canti and the nearby Piazza Pretoria (▷ 29), or Taormina's Corso Umberto I (▷ 50).

Shopping

Like the rest of Italy, Sicily is a great place for shopping. There are some department stores and supermarkets, but generally Sicilians prefer specialist shops with personalized service and street markets that are as colourful as they are entertaining. As for *Alta Moda* (High Fashion), Palermo was the birthplace of Domenico Dolce, who co-founded one of the world's most famous designer brands, Dolce & Gabbana.

Glorious Food

Extra virgin olive oil, hams, pungent cheeses, capers, pistachios, almonds, honey, chocolate, marzipan fruits, wines—the list of Sicilian gourmet foods seems endless. They make wonderful souvenirs, so evocative of this sun-drenched island. There are plenty of excellent delis and wine shops, not just in the main cities of Palermo and Catania, but also notably in Taormina, Cefalù, Ortygia and the Aeolian Islands. You will find markets in virtually every town—in the smaller ones they run once a week, usually on Thursday or Friday, while in the big cities they are open daily and are a huge attraction to locals and tourists alike.

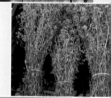

Good Buys

Among the best souvenirs are ceramics from Caltagirone and Sciacca, medieval-style marionettes from Palermo and lava trinkets from Etna. In Ortygia you'll find notebooks crafted from papyrus and gorgeously scented candles, lotions and potions.

IN VINO VERITAS

Sicily has more vineyards than any other region of Italy. Local wines range from the robust ruby-black Nero d'Avola to the rich, complex wines of volcanic Etna; from the famous Marsala (sweet or dry) to the honeyed Malvasia from the Aeolian Islands. It is always better to buy in specialized wine shops *(enoteche)*, where you can also taste the fruits of the vine.

Shopping options range from sweet treats and local wines to herbs and colourful sun hats

Sicily by Night

Sicilians know how to enjoy themselves, whether taking the time-honoured *passeggiata* (evening stroll) or dancing the night away at a throbbing city club. In the villages the local bar is the meeting place, where all the generations happily congregate. In bigger towns you'll often find venues hosting live music by international performers.

Alfresco Partying

The season of parties in open-air venues begins after Easter. The residents of Palermo head for Mondello, their seaside backyard, and, after the obligatory *passeggiata*, congregate around Piazza Mondello before heading off to the alfresco discos. In central Palermo the streets around Via Principe di Belmonte, Via Candelai and piazzas Castelnuovo and Verdi are like one big nightclub, peppered with cafés, bars, restaurants and live music venues. In Taormina, Sicily's 'bohemian capital', the action revolves around the Corso Umberto I, where there are plenty of bars and clubs. And in June the cinema festival comes to Taormina, along with its entourage of celebrities.

Other Hot Spots

Catania is famous for its lively nightlife, catering for its large university population, and is also becoming a top venue for jazz. Resorts in the provinces of Agrigento, Trapani and Siracusa are popular centres of nightlife, much of which takes place in seaside villages along the coast.

Nightlife ranges from the evening passeggiata to enjoying drinks in a bar or open-air café, or clubbing

---

TOP FESTIVALS

Taormina's spectacular Teatro Greco is the setting for plays and concerts from June to August. Agrigento's Valle dei Templi is the backdrop to ancient plays and classical concerts in summer and Siracusa's Parco Archeologico is the stage for the summer Festival of Classical Theatre. At other times, you are virtually guaranteed that a *festa* will be happening somewhere, culminating in feasting, merriment and a splendid firework display.

Eating Out

Greek, Norman, Spanish, Arabic and Italian are the main culinary influences in Sicily, but you will rarely eat anything that hasn't been produced within a few kilometres of where you're sitting.

Trattoria or *Ristorante*?
In the old days, the trattoria and *osteria* were more basic and less formal than the *ristorante*. Distinctions have now been blurred and some trattorias now count among Sicily's smartest restaurants. Then there are *ristoranti-pizzerie*, which serve pizzas and often pasta, fish and meat, too. Lunch is usually served from noon to 3.30pm and dinner from 7 to 11pm. For snacks, look for a *tavola calda* (hot table) that sells fast foods such as pizzas and *arancini*— stuffed, fried rice balls. Like all Italians, Sicilians dress up for dinner, and children are welcomed with open arms just about everywhere.

What's on the Menu
Meals begin with antipasti—a selection of cold meats, seafood and plump vegetables. This is followed by *il primo*, usually a pasta dish such as *pasta alla Norma*, made with aubergines, tomatoes and fresh ricotta, or *pasta con le sarde,* with sardines, anchovies and fennel. *Il secondo* could be fresh fish on the coast or aromatic cheeses and meats in the interior. Although Sicily is renowned for its *dolci* (desserts), you'll find a better selection in a *pasticceria* (patisserie) or you can treat yourself to a *gelato* in one of the numerous ice-cream parlours.

STREET FOOD
If you're in a hurry in Palermo, a cone of *calamaretti* (little squid) or *gamberetti fritti* (fried shrimp) with a squeeze of juicy Sicilian lemon is perfect to eat on the hoof as you weave through the fascinating markets. In Catania you can snack on food sold from carts, such as *alivi cunzati* (olives with chilli and pickles) or *calia e simenza* (roasted pumpkin seeds and chickpeas).

From top: Arancini are popular; a restaurant sign in Erice; cheese for sale; delicious ice creams

Restaurants by Cuisine

There are restaurants to suit all tastes and budgets in Sicily, with the emphasis on locally sourced and produced food. On this page the restaurants are listed by cuisine. For a more detailed description of each of our recommendations, see Sicily by Area.

FINE DINING

Al Duomo (▷ 60)
Al Fogher (▷ 92)
Bye Bye Blues (▷ 44)
Casa Grugno (▷ 60)
Don Camillo (▷ 78)
Duomo (▷ 78)
Hostaria del Vicolo (▷ 92)
Monte San Giuliano (▷ 106)
Oinos (▷ 78)
Ostaria del Duomo (▷ 44)

FISH AND SEAFOOD

Al Covo dei Beati Paoli (▷ 34)
Al Gabbiano (▷ 44)
La Bettola dal 1972 (▷ 106)
Trattoria dei Templi (▷ 92)

ITALIAN

Centrale (▷ 92)
Osteria del Campanile (▷ 60)

LIGHT BITES

Antica Caffè Spinnato (▷ 34)
Antica Focacceria San Francesco (▷ 34)
Caffè del Duomo (▷ 60)
Putia da Aldo (▷ 60)

PASTICCERIE/ GELATERIE

Bar Gelateria Costanzo (▷ 78)
Caffè Marro (▷ 92)
Cappello (▷ 34)
Gelati Divini (▷ 78)
Ilardo (▷ 34)
Pasticceria Gelateria di Catalano (▷ 92)

Pasticceria Grammatico (▷ 106)

RISTORANTI-PIZZERIE

Al Capo (▷ 106)
Il Barocco (▷ 78)
La Botte (▷ 60)
Granduca (▷ 60)

TRADITIONAL SICILIAN

Ai Lumi (▷ 106)
Al Cancelleto Verde (▷ 34)
La Brace (▷ 44)
Cantina Siciliana (▷ 106)
Dietro La Cattedrale (▷ 34)
Nangalarruni (▷ 44)
Ristorante Eubes (▷ 106)
La Scala (▷ 78)
Stella (▷ 34)
Taverna del Pavone (▷ 44)
Trattoria Garibaldi (▷ 106)
Trattoria La Ruota (▷ 92)

If You Like...

However you'd like to spend your time in Sicily, these ideas should help you tailor your ideal visit. Each sight or listing has a fuller write-up elsewhere in the book.

DIGGING UP THE PAST

Reconstruct gladiatorial combat at the magnificent Taormina Greek Theatre (▷ 51).
See the building blocks of Siracusa at the Parco Archeologico della Neapolis (▷ 68).
Visit the city of the dead among 8,000 mummified corpses at Palermo's 16th-century Catacombe dei Cappuccini (▷ 25).
Climb Cefalù's rock, La Rocca (278m/912ft), which is topped by a Norman castle (▷ 38).
Meander among the majestic temples and acropolis of the once-great Selinunte (▷ 102).

LA DOLCE VITA

Taste the world-famous pastries of Erice's Pasticceria Grammatico (▷ 96, 104, 106).
Indulge in some sweet moments at Monreale's Dolci Momenti (▷ 43).
Sip the fabled wines of Marsala (▷ 106).
Slurp a delicious rose *gelato* at Bar Gelateria Costanzo, Noto's famous ice-cream parlour (▷ 78).
Tuck into the antipasti buffet at Enna's Centrale restaurant (▷ 92).

La Rocca stands guard over the beach at Cefalù (above); Taormina's Teatro Greco (top)

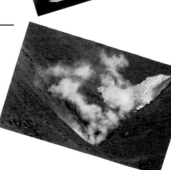

EARTH-SHATTERING EVENTS

Get up close to Etna, Europe's highest volcano (▷ 49, 57).
Look down into the mouth of Etna's newest crater, Bocca Nuova, a result of the 2006 eruption (▷ 49).
Say hello to the smiling elephant carved from lava in the fountain of Catania's Piazza Duomo (▷ 56).

Marsala wine, a Sicilian speciality (above top); smouldering Mount Etna (above right)

HAVING FUN WITH THE KIDS

Get a sea view of Mediterranean and tropical aquatic life at Siracusa's Acquario (▷ 73).

Pull a string at the best marionette theatre in the world at Palermo's Museo Internazionale delle Marionette Antonio Pasqualino (▷ 29).

Walk with the dinosaurs at Etnaland, with prehistoric models, water fun and shows (▷ 52).

Enjoy a day at the beach on the beautiful sands of Giardini-Naxos (▷ 52).

Fishing boats at Castellammare del Golfo (above)

THE NATURAL WORLD

View the dizzy depths of the great ravine Gole dell'Alcantara—just don't forget some warm clothes (▷ 53).

Commune with nature in Sicily's greatest national park, Parco Naturale delle Madonie (▷ 41).

See the resident flamingoes on the lagoons of the Riserva Naturale di Vendicari (▷ 74).

Explore Sicily's very first nature reserve, the Riserva Naturale dello Zingaro (▷ 100).

PEOPLE-WATCHING

Stroll around Palermo's Quattro Canti and the nearby Piazza Pretoria (▷ 29).

Enjoy a coffee on the terrace of one of the bars in Cefalù's Piazza Duomo (▷ 38, 39).

See and be seen in Taormina's Corso Umberto I, the focus of the town's *passeggiata* (▷ 50).

Join locals and visitors strolling in the Piazza Duomo in Catania (▷ 56), enjoying its baroque elegance.

Taking photos at the Gole dell'Alcantara (above)

A shop on Taormina's Corso Umberto I displays its intriguing items outside

EXPLORING UNDERWATER

Go diving from the Cetaria Diving Centre at
Scopello, Castellammare del Golfo (▷ 105).
Choose a diving course from a wide selection offered at Gorgonia Blu Diving, Marsala
(▷ 105).
The coastal area of Zingaro Nature Reserve
has excellent diving facilities (▷ 100).

*From top: the coastline at
Scopello, in the Riserva
Naturale dello Zingaro; the
church of San Giovanni
degli Eremiti, in Palermo; the
Madonie mountains*

WORKS OF ART AND ANTIQUITY

Get face to face with the male equivalent of
the *Mona Lisa* in Cefalù (▷ 38).
See the prized fourth-century BC bronze
Il Satiro Danzante (the Dancing Satyr) at Mazara
del Vallo (▷ 98).
Be moved by the exquisite beauty of the life-
sized fifth-century BC marble statue *Il Giovinetto
di Mozia (Young Man of Mozia)* at the Whitaker
Museum of Mozia (▷ 99).

WALKS OF DISCOVERY

Explore the rich city life of Palermo and
discover its fascinating past (▷ 30).
Enjoy great shopping as you wander through the
lava city of Catania, with its famous opera house
and lively markets (▷ 56).
**Immerse yourself in the classical monu-
ments,** medieval *palazzi* and baroque churches of
Ortygia, Siracusa's island heart (▷ 75).
Lose yourself in Enna's maze of streets in
this hilltop fortress town (▷ 88).

SPECTACULAR SCENERY

Set sail to see the dramatic firework
display given by Stromboli's volcano
(▷ 48).
Drive through the Madonie
mountains (▷ 42) or up Mount
Etna (▷ 57).
Enjoy some of Sicily's finest views on a
circular walk around Enna (▷ 87, 88).

ESSENTIAL SICILY IF YOU LIKE...

Sicily by Area

Sicily's vibrant capital is a frenetic bustle of pedestrians and traffic. This is bolstered in summer by hordes of visitors seeking out the historic treasures of a city that's been the focal point of civilization in Sicily for 2,500 years.

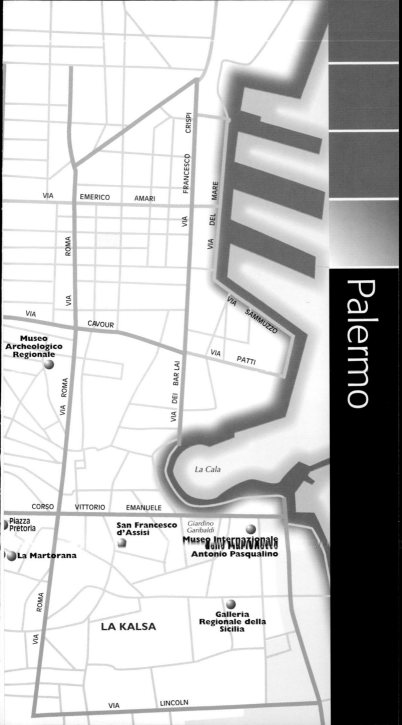

Cappella Palatina

Frescoes (left), the shimmering ceiling (middle) and the mosaic floor (right)

TOP 25

THE BASICS

✚ a4
✉ Piazza Indipendenza
☎ 091 626 2833
🕐 Mon–Sat 8.30–12, 2–5, Sun 8.30–10, 11–12.30
🍴 Restaurants in the piazza outside
🚌 104, 105, 108, 109, 110, 118, 304, 309
♿ None
💷 Moderate

HIGHLIGHTS

● The Easter candlestick, carved with more than 100 intricate animal forms
● The mosaic of Adam and Eve with the forbidden fruit in their mouths
● The Royal Apartments within the palace, with the superbly decorated bedroom of the King

TIP

● Don't miss the ceiling in the central nave, which is a masterpiece by Islamic artists depicting scenes of daily life.

Deep in the Palazzo dei Normanni, seat of the 12th-century Sicilian kings, the jewel-like Cappella Palatina is Palermo's greatest treasure.

Mix 'n' match The ceiling is Arabic, the mosaics Greek and Italian, the pulpit and huge paschal candelabrum are Norman, while the Romans laid the intricate pavements. The 'palace chapel', located within the Palazzo dei Normanni, was built between 1132–43 by King Roger II of Sicily for his private devotions and as a celebration of architectural and theological diversity. The dais behind the nave was where Roger sat during services.

Layout Shimmering with colour and bathed in reflected light, the chapel is divided by antique columns into a nave and two side aisles. At the east end is the sanctuary, comprising three apses, each decorated with mosaics.

Glittering mosaics The earliest of the mosaics were by Byzantine craftsmen. The central figure in the sanctuary is Christ the Pantocrator, who is depicted enthroned as the sagacious ruler of the universe. He is flanked on one side by a mosaic of the Madonna and Child and on the other by a depiction of the Nativity. Elsewhere in the chapel there are imaginative mosaics of scenes from the Old Testament, including the Creation, Noah and the Ark and the Fall of Man. There are also Islamic carvings—including a tableau representing a picnic in a harem.

Catacombe dei Cappuccini

TOP
25

Clothed corpses in the catacomb—not a sight for the faint-hearted

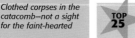

The sight of 8,000 mummified corpses in a variety of postures—horizontal, diagonal, upright hanging from walls—is a macabre sensation.

Welcome to the hereafter The Catacombe, at the Convento dei Cappuccini, has been in use since the 16th century, when the monks interred their dead brothers in stone corridors under the church and discovered the site had remarkable preservative qualities. Well-heeled local residents started to pay for their remains to be preserved in the Catacombe, dressed according to their wishes. By then, the process was more sophisticated, by means of dehydration and the use of chemicals. Mortified? You will be by the multitude of cadavers with gruesome expressions and deathly hair, along with many decayed well beyond recognition.

Social standing Bodies are located according to the social standing of the deceased, but they are also divided into groups of men, women, children, soldiers, virgins, monks and different professions. Many were famous in their day and it is said they include the Spanish painter Diego Velazquez, although his body is not signposted.

Sleeping Beauty The most recent, and saddest, corpse of the many infants in the Catacombe is of Rosalia Lombardo, who died aged two in 1920. She was preserved by a secret process, since lost, so perfectly that she seems to be merely sleeping.

THE BASICS

✠ Off a3
✉ Piazza Cappuccini 1
☎ 191 212 117
🕐 Mar–Oct daily 8.30–1, 2.30–6; Nov–Feb daily 9–12.30, 3–5.30. Closed public hols
🍴 Bars in nearby Via Cappuccini
🚌 327
♿ None
💶 Inexpensive

HIGHLIGHTS

● The clothes
● Rosalia Lombardo
● Priests in their robes, heads bowed and looking penitent
● The body of Giuseppe Tomasi, author of *Il Gattopardo (The Leopard)*

TIP

● Don't take in tow anyone who is squeamish about dead bodies. A visit here can be a bit gruelling, even for the non-squeamish.

PALERMO

★ **TOP 25**

La Cattedrale

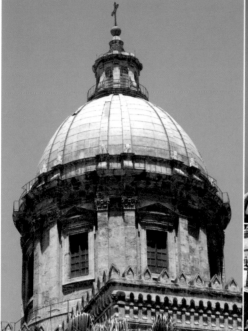

HIGHLIGHTS

- Gothic exterior
- Catalan south porch
- Treasury and Norman crown
- Crown of Constance of Aragon
- Crypt
- Four campaniles
- The Dome

TIP

- If you are pressed for time, catch a sightseeing bus–they all feature the cathedral as a major stop.

The golden bulk of Palermo's cathedral rises to one side of the arrow-straight Corso Vittorio Emanuele. Its architectural styles are a testament to changing rulers.

Beginnings The cathedral was founded in 1185 on the site of an earlier Byzantine structure that during Saracen times had been a mosque. It was the brainchild of an Englishman named Walter of the Mill who, as Archbishop of Palermo, was known as Gualtiero Offamiglio. Ambitious Walter rose from the ranks of tutor to the children of King William I—one of whom became William II—and the cathedral was meant to be his crowning glory. However, it wasn't completed until more than 200 years later, when the superb Catalan-Gothic triple-arched porch was finally finished in 1426.

Palermo's cathedral displays an enticing mix of architectural styles, with highlights including the Catalan-Gothic triple-arched porch (below) and the dome (far left)

Glimpses of the past Although eclipsed in beauty and grandeur by the rival cathedral at Monreale (▷ 40), Palermo's cathedral remains a fascinating study of architectural styles over the ages. The original building work, with its Moorish underlay, was given Gothic treatment in the 13th and 14th centuries, then the Spaniards came along and made their mark in the 15th century. Finally, between 1771 and 1809 the interior and exterior were overhauled in neoclassical style.

Royal resting place Its place in history is assured by its distinction as the resting place of Sicily's most famous royalty, including Roger II, his daughter Constance, Henry VI, Frederick II and his wife Constance of Aragon, and—the last to be buried in 1342—Peter II.

THE BASICS

www.cattedrale.palermo.it
✚ c3
✉ Piazza Cattedrale, Corso Vittorio Emanuele
☎ 191 334 373
🕐 Mon–Sat 8.30–5.30, Sun 8–1.30, 4–7. Closed during services
🚌 103, 104, 108, 110, 118, 139
♿ Fair
✋ Free, but donations are welcome; Crypt and Treasury inexpensive

More to See

GALLERIA REGIONALE DELLA SICILIA

Housed in the 1488 Palazzo Abatellis, this gallery does justice to its beautifully ornate surroundings. Sicily's finest art collection is spread across two floors crammed with paintings and sculptures. Among the most striking exhibits are Francesco Laurana's marble bust of Eleonora d'Aragona and a magnificent 15th-century fresco depicting *The Triumph of Death*.

➕ f4 ✉ Via Alloro 4 ☎ 191 263 0011
🕐 Tue, Thu, Sat, Sun 9–1, 3–7
🍴 Stella (nearby at Via Alloro 104; ▷ 34)
🚌 Tourist bus Linea A; 103, 105, 139
♿ Fair ✋ Expensive

LA MARTORANA AND SAN CATALDO CHURCHES

These dramatically contrasting city gems, founded in the 12th century, are in Piazza Bellini. La Martorana has colourful frescoes and an elegant bell tower. San Cataldo, with its three red domes, is on a bank above the piazza and is surrounded by palm trees. Inside it is quite plain, although the Arabic mosaic pavement is beautiful.

➕ d4 ✉ Piazza Bellini 3 ☎ La Martorana: 191 616 1692. San Cataldo: 338 722 8775
🕐 La Martorana: Mon–Sat 8–1, 3.30–7. San Cataldo: Mon–Sat 9.30–1, 3.30–6, Sun 9.30–1 🚌 Tourist bus Linea A; 101, 102, 103, 104 ♿ Few ✋ Moderate

MUSEO ARCHEOLOGICO REGIONALE

As well as being a splendid museum in its own right, the Museo Archeologico Regionale provides visitors with a great pointer to the sites in Sicily that are worth visiting. Its exhibits are a rich array of finds from various Neolithic, Carthaginian, Greek and Roman settlements on the island. Notable among these is the room devoted to treasures from the once-mighty Greek city of Selinunte (▷ 102).

➕ d2 ✉ Piazza Olivella 24 ☎ 191 611 6805 🕐 Tue–Sat 8.30–6.15, Sun 9–1
🍴 Bars in Piazza Verdi 🚌 101, 102, 103, 104, 107 ♿ Fair ✋ Moderate

An intricate mosaic of an angel in La Martorana

The Arab-Norman San Cataldo church, with its three red domes

MUSEO INTERNAZIONALE DELLE MARIONETTE ANTONIO PASQUALINO

www.museomarionettepalermo.it

Puppet theatre is a traditional form of Sicilian entertainment and this fascinating museum has some 3,500 exhibits, largely handmade and some very old. The locally produced figures, 80cm (31in) tall and dressed in rich costumes, evoke stories set in the age of chivalry, as do the shows that are staged at the museum. There are also some exotic puppets from the East.

➕ f4 ✉ Piazzetta Antonio Pasqualino 5 (parallel to Via Butera) ☎ 191 328 060
🕐 Mon–Sat 9–1, 3.30–8.30pm, Sun 9–1
🍴 Cafés in Piazza Marina 🚌 Tourist bus Linea A; 103, 105, 139, 824 ♿ Fair
✋ Visits free; shows expensive

PIAZZA PRETORIA

This square was once known as the Piazza of Shame because of its nude statues. It is dominated by a magnificent fountain that is adorned with the offending figures, along with water-spouting animals of white Carrara marble. The fountain was originally commissioned by a Tuscan nobleman, who then sold it to Palermo. Its somewhat chaotic design has been a controversial feature of the city since 1573.

➕ d4 🍴 Various restaurants nearby
🚌 Tourist bus Linea A; 101, 102, 103, 104
♿ Few

SAN FRANCESCO D'ASSISI

Home to a chapel that is the earliest example of Renaissance art in Sicily, the church of San Francesco d'Assisi dates back to the 13th century but is a comfortable mix of styles. Its statue of the Immaculate Conception plays a central role in a ceremony on 8 December, when Palermo's mayor prays for the Virgin to protect the city.

➕ e4 ✉ Piazza San Francesco d'Assisi
☎ 091 582 370 🕐 Daily 9–12, 4–6.30
🚌 Tourist bus Linea A; 101, 102 ♿ Few
✋ Free

Statues in the Museo Archeologico Regionale

This long-bearded statue is part of the Fontana Pretoria

The Heart of Palermo

This walk takes you past great markets, flamboyant baroque churches, the city Opera House and plenty of shops.

DISTANCE: 3km (2 miles) **ALLOW:** 2 hours

START

PIAZZA G. CESARE
🗺 d5 🚌 101, 102, 109, 139

END

PIAZZA G. CESARE

1 With your back to Stazione Centrale, cross Piazza G. Cesare and head down Via Roma, built in 1922 to connect the old city with Via della Libertà.

2 Continue along Via Roma, crossing Corso Vittorio Emanuele, and take the steps down to the right into the Vuccaria market, Palermo's most atmospheric market, offering fresh produce, fish, meat and spices.

3 Follow the market street of Via Maccheronai along to your left to emerge on Piazza San Domenico. Turn left, cross Via Roma and walk up Via Bandiera to Via Maqueda.

4 Cross Via Maqueda and walk up Via Sant'Agostino and through the Capo Market. As well as offering fresh produce, the Capo also sells DVDs, household goods and jewellery.

8 You'll soon notice the Piazza Pretoria (▷ 29) across the road on your left as you walk past the entrance of the Law Faculty of Palermo University. Via Maqueda will lead you back to Piazza G. Cesare and Stazione Centrale.

7 Cross the road to visit the baroque church of San Giuseppe dei Teatini and then continue along Via Maqueda.

6 In front of the Teatro Massimo (▷ 33) turn right onto Via Maqueda, one of the city's most historic streets. Continue to the Quattro Canti, the crossroads of the four old city quarters.

5 At the top of Via Sant'Agostino, turn right and walk along, past the Madonna della Mercè, to Via Volturno. Turn right and walk towards the monstrously large Teatro Massimo, the town's top opera and ballet venue.

WALK

PALERMO

Shopping

BARBISIO

www.barbisiopalermo.it
Palermo's premier men's outfitter has everything the design-conscious male could want. It stocks anything from beautifully tailored suits by Versace, Borsalino and Ungaro to casual wear from Missoni and Paolo da Ponte.

➕ d1 ✉ Piazza Marchese di Regalmici 8 ☎ 091 588 774 🚌 101, 102, 103, 104, 124

CAMBRIA

There are more than 100 cheeses from all over Sicily in this store, as well as a wide selection of cheeses from mainland Italy. You can also buy *salumi* (cold meats), oils and pasta. A speciality is pecorino and mountain cheeses from the Madonie.

➕ Off map ✉ Via Liguria 91 ☎ 091 517 791 🚌 101

CARNEVALISSIMO

Visiting this shop is an entertainment in itself, even if you don't intend to buy. It is wonderfully kitted out with costumes for babies, children and adults, with designs ranging from Ancient Rome via Disney to Rocky Horror.

➕ c2 ✉ Via Volturno 33 ☎ 091 585 787 🚌 101, 102, 103, 104, 124

CERAMICA DE SIMONE

You'll find pottery for all occasions, both practical and decorative, at the pick of the city's ceramic outlets.

➕ Off map ✉ Via Lanza di Scalea 698-700 ☎ 091 671 1005 🕔 Closed Sat, Sun 🚌 101

GIGLIO

www.giglio.com
Giglio stocks Italy's top designer labels, including Emporio Armani, Prada and Moschino. One of several Giglio shops around the Via della Libertà, this beautiful store specializes in sportswear and designer jeans.

➕ Off map ✉ Piazza A. Mordini 3 ☎ 091 625 7727 🚌 101, 102

GUIDO COSENTINO

This long-established store in the heart of Palermo is a treasure trove of jewellery, silver, crystal and porcelain.

CITY SHOPPING

As befits a capital city, Palermo has plenty of shopping opportunities. Sicilian souvenirs include ceramics, lace, puppets, miniature Sicilian carts and the traditional *frutta martorana*—jewel-coloured marzipan sweets. Look, too, for chestnut wood and rush baskets and intricately crafted wrought-iron items. As well as a large variety of local markets, there are shops that are a delight to visit, even without any intention of buying.

➕ d2 ✉ Via Cavour 117 ☎ 091 328 362 🚌 101, 102, 104

LINA D'ANTONA

Homecraft enthusiasts will love this Aladdin's cave of old-fashioned haberdashery, including beautiful ribbons, buttons, threads, silks, belts and laces.

➕ d3 ✉ Via Maqueda 413 ☎ 091 588 895 🚌 101, 102, 103, 104, 124

MANFREDI BARBERA E FIGLI

www.oliobarbera.com
It would be sacrilege to leave Sicily without some olive oil—and this is the place to get it. The family-run business, founded in 1894, produces some of the island's finest oils. Staff will happily help you choose the style and strength—from light and delicate *extra vergine* (virgin) to peppery and aromatic.

➕ d1 ✉ Via Emerico Amari ☎ 091 582 900 🚌 101, 102, 104

LA RINASCENTE

www.rinascente.it
This glamorous department store opened in spring 2010. Five floors are devoted to fashion, accessories, beauty, houseware, design and gourmet food. The Food Hall, bars and restaurants are open until midnight.

➕ e3 ✉ Via Roma (after 9pm use entrance in Piazza San Domenico) ☎ 091 601 7811 🚌 101, 104, 107

Entertainment and Activities

ASSOCIAZIONE FIGLI D'ARTE CUTICCHIO
www.figlidartecuticchio.com
Enjoy great family entertainment at a traditional Sicilian puppet theatre. The performances are in Italian, but you don't need to be a linguist to enjoy the action.
🔲 d2 ✉ Via Bara Olivella 95 ☎ 091 323 400 🚌 101, 102, 103, 104, 124

I CANDELAI
www.candelai.it
Well-established on the Palermo night scene, this club is still one of Palermo's hottest venues. Live gigs, performing arts and DJ sessions keep the place buzzing till late.
🔲 c3 ✉ Via dei Candelai 65 ☎ 091 327 151 🕐 Daily 9pm–3am 🚌 103, 104

LA CUBA
www.lacuba.com
It's glamorous at this lounge, café and club between the Parco della Favorita and Giardino Inglese and the code is definitely to dress up. There's a wine/cocktail bar, a brasserie and a delightful garden
🔲 Off map ✉ Viale Francesco Scaduto 12 ☎ 091 309 201 🕐 Mon–Sat 7pm–2am, Sun noon–2am 🚌 101

KURSAAL KALHESA
www.kursaalkalhesa.it
This wine bar is a great spot to begin the evening, on opulent sofas under the vaults of a medieval palazzo or in the courtyard with a cocktail in hand. Musical events are staged. There's a restaurant upstairs.
🔲 Off map ✉ Via Foro Umberto Primo 1 21 ☎ 091 616 0050, 091 616 2111 🕐 Tue–Fri 12–3, 6–1.30, Sat, Sun noon–1.30am 🚌 Tourist bus Linea A; 103, 105, 139, 824

TEATRO BIONDO
www.teatrobiondo.it
This theatre in the centre of town offers a variety of plays, including home-grown comedies and dramas and locally adapted productions of Shakespeare tragedies.
🔲 d3 ✉ Via Roma 258 ☎ 091 743 4311 🚌 101, 102, 104, 107, 124

TEATRO FRANCO ZAPPALÀ
www.teatrofrancozappala.com
Named after its artistic director, this attractive

theatre specializes in its own Sicilian-dialect productions. If your Sicilian isn't up to it, skip the drama and try to catch a variety show, operetta or opera.
🔲 Off map ✉ Via Autonomia Siciliana ☎ 091 543 380, 091 362 764 🚌 101

TEATRO LIBERO
www.teatroliberopalermo.it
Founded in the 1960s, this is a theatre for true lovers of dramatic art and the Italian language. It specializes in avant garde productions.
🔲 e4 ✉ Piazza Marina ☎ 091 617 4040 🚌 103, 105

TEATRO MASSIMO
www.teatromassimo.it
Catching a performance at Palermo's principal arts venue is a major highlight of any trip to Sicily. Opera, ballet and concerts are staged year-round.
🔲 d2 ✉ Piazza G. Verdi ☎ 091 605 3111 🚌 101, 102, 104, 107

TEATRO POLITEAMA GARIBALDI
www.orchestrasinfonica siciliana.it
Home of the island's major symphony orchestra, the Orchestra Sinfonica Siciliana, this 18th-century theatre stages year-round performances of classical music concerts.
🔲 d1 ✉ Via Turati 2 ☎ 091 588 001 🚌 101, 102, 103, 806, 812

Restaurants

AL CANCELLETTO VERDE (€€)

www.alcancellettoverde.it
Typical Sicilian fare is on offer here at a reasonable price. The food is diligently prepared and cheerfully served in neat and colourful surroundings.

➕ d1 ✉ Via R. Wagner 14 ☎ 091 320 537 🕒 Daily lunch and dinner 🚌 103, 104

AL COVO DEI BEATI PAOLI (€€)

www.alcovodeibeatipaoli.com
Enjoy excellent seafood and a great atmosphere in one of Palermo's most pleasant piazzas, with a wide menu to choose from.

➕ e4 ✉ Piazza Marina 50 ☎ 091 616 6634 🕒 Daily dinner 🚌 103, 105

ANTICA CAFFÉ SPINNATO (€€)

This is a good choice for day or night, with a garden for alfresco lunches and a piano bar for romantic dinners. The specialities are pastries, almond biscuits and ice creams, though the delicatessen bar is also a treat. It's all beautifully presented in an old-world Sicilian setting, with warm hospitality.

➕ d1 ✉ Piazza Castelnuovo 16 ☎ 091 329 220 🕒 Daily lunch and dinner 🚌 101, 102, 106

ANTICA FOCACCERIA SAN FRANCESCO (€)

www.afsf.it
This traditional eating place, established in 1834 and decked out with marble-topped tables, offers an authentic taste of Palermo. Here you'll find the uniquely Sicilian idea of fast food, with all the convenience but no lack of flavour or atmosphere.

➕ e4 ✉ Via Alessandra Paternostro 58 ☎ 091 320 264 🕒 Daily 10am to midnight 🚌 103, 104, 105

CAPPELLO (€)

www.pasticceriacappello.it
Renowned for its chocolate-based dishes, this superb pasticceria also has a vast range of pastries and cakes. Try the typically Palermitan rich cake cassata Siciliana.

➕ a3 ✉ Via Colonna Rotta 68 ☎ 091 489 601 🕒 Daily lunch and dinner 🚌 103, 104, 108, 110, 118, 139

DIETRO LA CATTEDRALE (€€)

Over and above its perfect location for visitors to the cathedral, Dietro la Cattedrale ('behind the cathedral') offers good prices and a menu that's based on the best available produce of the day.

➕ b-c3 ✉ Piazza Santi 40 Martiri alla Guilla ☎ 091 588 755 🕒 Daily 12–3, 7.30–11 🚌 103, 104, 108, 110, 118, 139

ILARDO (€)

Palermo's most famous gelateria, founded in the 1880s, offers a huge range of ice creams, as well as water ices.

➕ f4 ✉ Foro Italico 11-12 ☎ 091 616 4413 🕒 Daily noon–2am 🚌 101, 102, 103, 104, 107

STELLA (€€–€€€)

Innovative dishes sit alongside traditional Sicilian fare on the menu of this immensely popular restaurant, in a palm-lined courtyard. Try the sarde a beccafico—sardines stuffed with spiced breadcrumbs and rolled up to resemble the little 'warbler' bird (beccafico).

➕ e4 ✉ Via Alloro 104 ☎ 091 616 1136 🕒 Daily lunch and dinner 🚌 103, 104

Within easy reach of Palermo are Cefalù, one of Sicily's loveliest towns, Mondello, with Monte Pellegrino as a backdrop, and Solunto, with its ancient ruins. See the island's most glittering mosaics at Monreale, or visit its greatest National Park, the Parco Naturale delle Madonie.

0   10 km
0   5 miles

Isole Eolie

Cefalù

Golfo di Termini Imerese

Capo Plaia

Sant'
Ambrogio

Capo Raisigerbi

Finale

Campofelice
di Roccella

A20

Lascari

Pollina

Termini Imerese

Gratteri

927

Buonfornello

Pizzo
Sant'Angelo

Portella di
Montenero

Borrello

1223

1326

Isnello

Pizzo Votturo

Monte San Calogero

Collesano

Mongerati

Castelbuono

Sciara

Cerda

808

*Parco Regionale
delle Madonie*

S Mauro
Castelverde

1346

Monte d'Oro

Piano Battaglia

Madonie

Geraci
Siculo

Timpa del Grillo

Monte-
maggiore
Belsito

Aliminusa

Marini

1912

901

Monte San
Salvatore

Portella Pizzo Cosimo
Mandarini

1145

A19

Scillato

Petralia
Sottana

Gangi

Monte Roccelito

Polizzi

Nociazzi

1002

Generosa

Selafani Bagni

Caltavuturo

Petralia Soprana

Pizzo
Conca

Calcarelli

Fasano

1332

Alia

Castellana
Sicula

Pianello

Verdi

Monte Zimmara

999

Portella
Mangiante

Blufi

Bompietro

San Tignino

Masseria
Xireni

Casalgiordana

Marcato
Bianco

Valledolmo

1042

Portella della
Signo

Monte Catuso

Resuttano

Alimena

Tudia

Portella di Morto

Portella
Recattivo

Recattivo

951

Monte
Chibbò

Cefalù

Dazzling white houses nestle up to the waterfront at scenic Cefalù

THE BASICS

www.cefalu-tour.pa.it;
www.cefaluinforma.it

➕ K2

ℹ Corso Ruggero 77, tel
0921 421050; Mon–Sat 8–8

🍴 Al Gabbiano
(▷ 44; €€)

🚌 From Palermo and
inland towns of the Madonie

🚉 Cefalù

Museo Mandralisca
www.museomandralisca.it

✉ Via Mandralisca 13

🕐 Daily 9–1, 3–7

♿ Moderate

HIGHLIGHTS

● Antonello da Messina's
Portrait of an Unknown Man
● La Rocca
● Beaches

TIPS

● The best time to climb La
Rocca is early morning or
early evening. Wear walking
boots and take water.
● The town is within reach of
great walks in the Madonie
mountains to the south.

Cradled between the mountains and coastline, guarded by a castle, this is one of Sicily's most picturesque towns.

Norman Conquest Although founded in Greek times, Cefalù later became a pet project for the Norman King Roger II (1130–54). From the beautifully preserved historic centre, medieval streets wind down to the long sandy beach where Roger II's ship was washed ashore, remarkably almost unscathed. Today he would find a jostling hive of beachside activity in August, but you can escape the hordes by climbing the castle-topped rock, La Rocca.

La Rocca For spectacular views, take the steep steps from Piazza Garibaldi, signposted Accesso alla Rocca, up to the vast rock (278m/912ft) that stands sentinel over the town. The ascent takes around an hour and you'll pass the ruins of the fifth-century BC Tempio di Diana (Temple of Diana). At the top there are Arabic and medieval fortifications, as well as wonderful views, stretching across from Palermo in the west to Capo d'Orlando in the east.

Enigmatic smile Within the town is the golden Duomo (▷ 39) and the Museo Mandralisca, whose great highlight is Antonello da Messina's *Portrait of an Unknown Man* (c.1460). Da Messina (1430–79) was Sicily's most eminent artist and this painting is his earliest known work, depicting the subject's sly, enigmatic gaze. At one time it was used as a cabinet door!

Cefalù: Duomo

Christ Pantocrator mosaic (left); the cathedral's twin towers (middle); a view towards the sea (right)

The landmark twin towers of Cefalù's cathedral, tight against the soaring La Rocca, are visible from miles around.

Fortress The building of Roger II's cathedral started in 1131 in gratitude for his safe deliverance to Cefalù's beach after a tempest. Austere and reminiscent of a fortress on the outside, it was designed to be a testament to Roger's power as the newly crowned King of Sicily and to demonstrate his might in the power struggle with Pope Innocent II. By the time of his death in 1154 it was still unfinished, but work continued until 1267, when it was finally consecrated.

Inside From the Piazza Duomo, steps lead to the arched entrance and cool, dark interior of one of Sicily's most perfect Norman churches. The nave is lined with 16 Roman columns taken from an ancient Temple of Diana—for this was originally a Roman site.

Glistening mosaics As your eyes become accustomed to the gloom, you will see the Byzantine mosaics dominating the apse, all set against a gold background. The figure of Christ the Pantocrator towers above, the open Bible in his left hand with the Latin inscription 'I am the light of the world: whoever follows me will never walk in darkness…' (John 8:12). These stunning mosaics, also depicting the Virgin, angels and saints, date to 1148–70 and were created by Greek master craftsmen, pre-dating those at Monreale by 40 years.

THE BASICS

✚ K2
✉ Piazza del Duomo
☎ 0921 922021
🕐 Apr–Sep daily 8–12, 3.30–7; Oct–Mar daily 8–12, 3.30–5 (closed during church services). Cloister generally daily 10–1, 3–4
🍴 Ostaria del Duomo (▷ 44; €€)
♿ Poor access via steps
💷 Free (donations welcome). Cloister inexpensive
❓ Occasional concerts—details from tourist office

HIGHLIGHTS

● Byzantine mosaics
● Christ Pantocrator
● Sixteen Roman columns
● Statue of the Madonna, by Antonello Gagini (16th century)
● Cloister (Chiostro)

TIP

● To see the facade shimmering in golden light, visit in the late afternoon.

Monreale: Duomo

TOP 25

Christ watches over his flock (left); inside and outside the cathedral (middle and right)

THE BASICS

www.cattedraledi
monreale.it
✚ G2
✉ Piazza Duomo
☎ 091 640 4413. Cloister
091 640 4403
🕐 Daily 8.30–12.30, 3.30–
6. Cloister daily 9–6.30
🍴 Taverna del Pavone
(▷ 44; €€)
🚌 389 from Palermo
(Piazza dell'Indipendenza)
♿ Good
🎟 Free. Treasury and
terrace moderate. Cloister
expensive

HIGHLIGHTS

● Bronze door created by
Bonnano Pisano (creator of
the Leaning Tower of Pisa)
● Mosaics
● Royal tombs
● Views from the roof
● Cloister and fountain

TIP

● The town of Monreale is
well worth exploring.

In the hills overlooking the Golden Shell valley, this sublime Norman cathedral has an interior smothered in mosaics.

Beginnings Monreale's cathedral was commissioned in 1174 by William II, whose avowed intent was to outdo the opulent Cappella Palatino, in Palermo (▷ 24), built by his grandfather Roger II, and to show off the magnificence of his kingdom. The result was a sumptuous fusion of western and eastern influences, with no expense spared.

Rich mosaics Second only in size to Istanbul's Basilica of Saint Sofia, the mosaic cycle covers almost 8,000sq m (86,111sq ft). Embellished with more than two tons of pure gold, these are Italy's richest and best-preserved Byzantine mosaics. Around 130 scenes from the Old and New Testament are displayed. Gazing down from the ceiling of the main apse is the exquisite Christ the Pantocrator, dominating the whole interior and giving the optical illusion of looking into your eyes, wherever you stand.

Cloister To the right of the cathedral is the exquisite 12th-century Benedictine Chiostro (Cloister). It is framed by 228 inlaid columns, each gloriously sculpted or richly gilded with mosaics depicting scenes varying from biblical and classical themes to animals, birds and monsters. The garden is a shady oasis of olives and bay trees with a fountain, shaped like a palm tree, where William II would wash.

More to See

BAGHERIA

Bagheria lies on the southern slopes of Monte Catalfano. In Piazza Garibaldi, the bizarre Villa Palagonia (open daily) was commissioned by the Prince of Palagonia in 1715 and its gardens are full of grotesque statues said to be caricatures of his unfaithful wife's many lovers.

H2 Restaurant and pizzeria near Villa Palagonia From Palermo Bagheria

MONDELLO

The Palermitans' favourite beach is 11km (7 miles) north of Palermo, round the looming bulk of Monte Pellegrino. The sandy beach stretches for 2km (over a mile). In summer it hosts open-air discos.

H2 Bye Bye Blues (▷ 44; €€€) 806 (also 833 in summer)

MONTE PELLEGRINO

Monte Pellegrino (606m/1,988ft) forms a spectacular backdrop to Palermo. Near the top is the Santuario di Santa Rosalia.

H2 812 from Palermo

MONTI MADONIE

www.parcodellemadonie.it

The mountains south of Cefalù are home to the Parco Naturale delle Madonie. Sicily's greatest national park rises to 1,900m (5,700ft) and covers 39,679ha (98,049 acres).

L3 Corso Paolo Agliati 16, Petralia Sottana, tel 0921 684011; Mon–Fri 9.30–1.30, 3.30–6.30 From Cefalù to Madonie villages For a drive, ▷ 42

SOLUNTO

These ancient ruins are spectacularly perched on Monte Catalfano, overlooking the sea and the fishing village of Porticello. The site was known as Solus to the Phoenician settlers in the eighth century BC. The Romans renamed it Soluntum in the third century BC. Highlights include the mosaics, Gymnasium and theatre ruins.

H2 091 904 557 Mon–Sat 9–6, Sun 9–1 Take a picnic; good fish restaurants in Porticello To Santa Flavia-Solunto-Porticello, then 30-minute walk None Moderate

Having fun on Mondello beach, with Monte Pellegrino in the background

Drive Through the Madonie Mountains

Experience one of Sicily's most beautiful mountain areas, with its spellbinding scenery and picturesque little hill towns.

DISTANCE: 135km (84 miles) **ALLOW:** 7 hours (including stops)

START

CEFALÙ ✚ K2

END

CEFALÙ

❶ Drive east along the coast towards Messina on the SS113. After 8km (5 miles) turn right, following the signs to Parco Naturale delle Madonie and the handsome town of Castelbuono, the area's 'capital'. Wander through Castelbuono's steep, rosy cobbled streets up to the medieval castle.

❷ Leave Castelbuono on the SS286 going south, following the signs to Geraci Siculo, taking you high into the mountains. Visit the old town centre for the spectacular views.

❸ Keep on the SS286 south to the junction with the SS120 and bear left onto it, then turn right for Petralia Soprana. This is among the Madonie's highest, most picturesque villages. Take advantage of the viewpoint near the Madonna di Loreto church.

❹ Fork right to Petralia Sottana, standing atop a green hill, then follow the signs to Collesano, Piano Battáglia and Piano dei Zucchi. This twisting road climbs through increasingly mountainous terrain to Piano Battáglia—a tiny ski resort with Swiss chalet-style houses.

❽ Follow the steeply descending road for the remaining 13km (8-mile) drive back to Cefalù. The road rejoins the main coastal road on the upper outskirts of Cefalù.

❼ Among cypress trees, the 18th-century sanctuary of Gibilmanna is the site of an image of the Madonna that is reputed to have performed miracles. It is especially popular with pilgrims on 8 September for the Festival of the Madonna. There are magnificent views over the mountains and sea and it's the perfect spot for a picnic.

❻ Leave Isnello and, after 3km (2 miles), turn left and follow the steeply descending road in the direction of Cefalù. After 9km (5.5 miles) the Santuario di Gibilmanna is off to the right.

❺ Follow the road to the right, following signs to Piano dei Zucchi and Isnello, and continue straight ahead. After 7km (4 miles) turn right to Isnello, a typical inland village.

Shopping

ANTARES

Browse here for beautifully crafted, colourful ceramics typical of the Madonie mountains area.
➕ K2 ✉ Via C.O. di Bordonaro 40/101, Cefalù ☎ 0921 420920

ARCHIMEDE

This art and fashion gallery, in glamorous surroundings, is guaranteed to make you want to part with your euros.
➕ K2 ✉ Via Archimede 17, Cefalù ☎ 0921 923974

DI CRISTINA

The classic Sicilian wine Nero d'Avola—full-bodied, ruby-black—and a host of Denominazione di Origine Controllata (DOC) offerings are all here, waiting to be uncorked.
➕ G2 ✉ Ctr Cambuca, Monreale ☎ 091 878 5044

DOLCI MOMENTI

Indulge in some sweet moments with a choice of divinely decadent *cannoli* oozing with ricotta or the sweet green cassata topped with a cherry, among countless others.
➕ G2 ✉ Via Venero 166, Monreale ☎ 0916 401099

ENOGASTRONOMIA BADALAMENTI

You can pick up a picnic at this well-stocked shop near the beach in Mondello. Cold meats, cheeses and many other delicacies, plus more than 1,000 wines, ensure a fine alfresco feast.
➕ H2 ✉ Viale Galatea 55, Mondello ☎ 091 982 0380

FIASCONARO

www.fiasconaro.com
I Sapori del Sole—the flavours of the sun—is the motto of this wonderful *pasticceria*/bar, which is devoted to sweet delights. *Torrone Siciliano* (soft nougat), *frutta martorana* (jewel-coloured marzipan fruits), cream of pistachios, hazelnuts and almonds are among the delectable offerings here.
➕ L3 ➕ Piazza Margherita 10, Castelbuono ➕ 0921 67713

KOSMOS DI ALBERTO CITRANO

This store offers beautiful leather accessories from designer names such as Coccinelle, Kipling and Tosca Blu.
➕ K2 ✉ Via Vittorio Emanuele 34, Cefalù (also Corso Ruggiero 36)
☎ 0921 922416

SAPORI DI SICILIA

Typical flavours and products of Sicily feature in this shop packed full with delicious goodies. Whether you're looking for cheese and wine or extra virgin olive oil and jams to take home, this is a gourmet's delight.
➕ K2 ✉ Via Vittorio Emanuele 93, Cefalù ☎ 0921 422871

SISLEY

www.francovirgagroup.it
On Cefalù's Via Roma, this is part of the Benetton Group, with the familiar affordable, casual fashions but in different colours and styles from those found elsewhere.
➕ K2 ✉ Via Roma 107, Cefalù ☎ 0921 923828

TORREFAZIONE SERIO

Close to Cefalù's Duomo, this long-established shop specializes in all kinds of delights, including freshly roasted coffee beans. Balsamic vinegar, olive oils, Sicilian wines, Marsala and all kinds of grappas are among the wonderfully aromatic tastes of this microcosm of Sicilian and Italian flavours.
➕ K2 ✉ Corso Ruggiero 120, Cefalù ☎ 0921 922348

PICNIC TIME
With so many beautiful places on your doorstep in Sicily, enjoy a picnic by stocking up in one of the many delis or markets. If you're driving, you'll see roadside stalls, manned by farmers, where you can pick up excellent-value freshly picked fruit, vegetables, cheese and honey. Some of Sicily's best honey is from the Madonie mountains—look for honey scented with orange blossom, thyme, chestnut flower or eucalyptus.

Restaurants

AL GABBIANO (€€)

A pleasant terrace looks out over the sea in one of Cefalù's prettiest and best seafront restaurants. Family-run and friendly, the speciality here is fish and seafood. Try, perhaps, a bowl of steaming *zuppa di cozze* (mussel soup) or, in the evening, very good pizzas.

✚ K2 ✉ Lungomare F. Giardina 17, Cefalù ☎ 0921 421495 🕐 Daily lunch and dinner. Closed Wed in winter

LA BRACE (€€)

www.ristorantelabrace.com
Dine on home-made pasta, fishy delights such as swordfish, or meat-based dishes including spicy chicken and rabbit. They're all served with imaginative flair in this cosy, atmospheric restaurant close to the Duomo. Leave room for the delicious puddings.

✚ K2 ✉ Via XXV Novembre 10 (off Corso Ruggiero), Cefalù ☎ 0921 423570 🕐 Wed–Sun lunch and dinner, Tue dinner. Closed 15 Dec–15 Jan

BYE BYE BLUES (€€€)

www.byebyeblues.it
This very chic restaurant has become the byword for fine dining in the Palermitans' seaside resort, Mondello. Professional sommelier Antonio Barraco's talents are matched by the culinary expertise of his wife, Patrizia. Expect traditional regional cuisine but with a modern, very inventive twist, served in elegant surroundings. Perhaps treat yourself to a five-course *menu degustazione* and be spoiled for choice with 350 different wine labels.

✚ H2 ✉ Via del Garofalo 23, Mondello ☎ 0916 841415 🕐 Wed–Mon dinner. Closed 10–31 Jan

NANGALARRUNI (€€)

www.hostariananagalarruni.it
This atmospheric 18th-century restaurant is hidden away in the heart of medieval Castelbuono.

Typical dishes of the area feature, such as wild mushrooms and wild boar, in season. If you have a sweet tooth, try the local speciality, *testa di turco* (▷ panel). There is also a splendid array of wine bottles on show.

✚ L3 ✉ Via delle Confraternite 5, Castelbuono ☎ 0921 671428 🕐 Thu–Tue lunch and dinner

OSTARIA DEL DUOMO (€€)

www.ostariadelduomo.com
Sit in one of Sicily's loveliest piazzas, gazing up at Cefalù's Duomo while enjoying local cooking with the accent on fish. Inside, sit under the vaulted ceiling in stylish surroundings. Although this is one of Cefalù's most sophisticated restaurants, prices are still reasonable.

✚ K2 ✉ Via Seminario 5, Cefalù ☎ 0921 421838 🕐 Tue–Sun 12–12. Closed mid-Nov to Feb

TAVERNA DEL PAVONE (€€)

www.tavernadelpavone.eu
A warm welcome awaits you at this family-run taverna, just a stone's throw from Monreale's famous Duomo. Typical Sicilian specialities feature on the menu, and you can sample very good home-made pasta.

✚ G2 ✉ Vicolo Pensato 18, Monreale ☎ 0916 406209 🕐 Tue–Sun lunch and dinner. Closed 2 weeks in Jun

The Northeast

This is the most popular corner of Sicily, attracting huge numbers to see Mount Etna, Europe's largest volcano and one of the world's most active. The region is also home to Catania and ancient Taormina.

Isola Stromboli & Panarea

San Bartolo
San Bartolo

Punta Bandiera

Capo Rasocolmo
Sparta
Castanea delle Furie
Capo Peloro
Sindaro Marina
Golfo di Milazzo
Ganzirri
Capo di Milazzo
Croce al Promontorio
Villafranca Tirrena
609 Monte Ciccia
Pace
Paradiso
Gesso
Golfo di Patti
Milazzo
Fossazzo
Saponara
Santa Maria delle Grazie
Scala
Torregrotta
Monforte San Giorgio
Saponara
Messina
Pace del Mela
Tremestieri
Capo Tindari
Tindari
Oliveri
Barcellona
Pozzo di Gotto
Santa Lucia del Mela
Pellegrino
Santo Stefano di Briga
Mili San Pietro
Moreri
Furnari
Castroreale
Altolia
Santa Maria
Basico
Milici
Bafia
Itala
Ali
Itala Marina
San Marco
1246 Monte Fossazza
Mandanici
Ali Terme
Montalbano Elicona
Novara di Sicilia
Rimiti
Antillo
Pagliara
Roccalumera
Furci Siculo
Portella Pertusa
1341 Monte Croce Mancina
Casalvecchio Siculo
Santa Teresa di Riva
Malvagna
Limina
Forza d'Agro
Capo Sant'Alesso
Francavilla di Sicilia
Mongiuffi
Letojanni
Montelaguardia
Alcantara
Melia
Mazzarò
Solicchiata
Gole dell' Alcantara
SS120
Taormina
Giardini-Naxos
Linguaglossa
Calatabiano
Capo Schiso
2049 Monte Nero
Piedimonte Etneo
Fiumefreddo di Sicilia
2414 Monte Pizzillo
Nunziata
Mascali
3323 Monte Etna
Fornazzo
Riposto
Zafferana Etnea
Giarre
Santa Venerina
Cantoniera d'Etna
Guardia
Fleri
Stazzo
Ragalna
Pedara
Acireale
Riviera dei Limoni
Mascalucia
Aci Catena
Valverde
San Giovanni Galermo
Aci Trezza
Riviera dei Ciclopi
Cannizzaro
Misterbianco
Motta Sant'Anastasia
Catania
San Giorgio
Lido di Plaia
SS417
Fontanarossa
Catania
Gornalunga
Golfo di Catania
Foce di Simeto
Vaccarizzo
Siracusa

0   20 km
0   10 miles

Q   R   S

Isole Eolie

A dramatic display from Stromboli's volcano (left); pretty Panarea island (right)

THE BASICS

🔳 Inset map
ℹ️ Via Vittorio Emanuele, 202, Lipari, tel 090 998 0095; Jul–Aug Mon–Sat 8–2, 4.30–10, Sun 8–2; Sep–Jun Mon–Fri 8–2, 4.30–7.30, Sat 8–2
🍴 E'Pulera (€€), Via Diana, Lipari
🚢 Frequent ferries and hydrofoils from the mainland to Lipari and Vulcano, and inter-island connections

HIGHLIGHTS

● The view from the lighthouse on Strombolicchio
● Sunsets
● Vulcano's Gran Cratere
● Archaeological sites on Lipari, Panarea and Filicudi
● Vulcano's mudbaths
● Displays of volcanic activity on Stromboli
● Lipari's beautiful Castello, the Episcopal palace and the cathedral

This tiny archipelago to the northeast of Sicily is named after King Aeolus who, in mythology, controlled the winds he kept hidden in one of the islands' caverns.

Isolated yet popular Even when the winds are hidden—as they seem to be in summer—the Aeolian Islands still evoke a sense of isolation. Yet in the last 50 years the islands have become a paradise for cyclists, underwater explorers, volcano-watchers and hikers.

Island attractions Lipari Island and Lipari town are at the heart of the islands' 6,000-year history, and home to the Museo Eoliano's collection of artefacts, some dating back to 3000BC. Nearby Vulcano has a lunar landscape, with traces of its 19th-century volcanic eruption and its legacy—sulphurous baths said to have healing powers. Stromboli's active volcano puts on a regular firework display, spewing lava down one side of its slopes. The isle of Salina has twin volcanic peaks and yet a rich green landscape, along with one of the most picturesque villages of the whole region.

Traffic-free The isle of Panarea doesn't have any cars, which may account for its rating as the prettiest of the Aeolians. It is surrounded by islets, which appear to be sitting in boiling water because of volcanic vents through which sulphuric gases escape. Filicudi and Alicudi are the least populous and least visited by tourists, but those who do visit claim they're the best.

Monte Etna

A crater view from high on Mount Etna (left); the snow-capped volcano looms over Taormina (right)

The brooding presence of Mount Etna, the smouldering giant that is the most active volcano in Europe, dominates eastern Sicily.

Many mouths Mount Etna is the highest volcano in Europe and among the most active in the world. The huge fuming cone, rising 3,323m (10,902ft) above sea level, has been rumbling for 3,500 years. For all its permanence, its landscape changes with every spew, belch and hiccup from its many mouths. The newest of these, Bocca Nuova, came to life in November 2006 when cascades of lava and fiery explosions engulfed the mountain. Further eruptions came in 2008 but, spectacular as they appeared, they were but a minor event compared with those of 2001 and 2002/3.

Nature trail The area is a regional park. The foothills are densely wooded with poplars, oaks, beech, birch and chestnuts, and the volcanic soils are perfect for fruit orchards, olive groves, nut plantations and vineyards.

Volcano visits A cable car from Rifugio Sapienza takes visitors to 2,500m (8,200ft) above sea level. From there you can take a tour in a four-by-four vehicle (▷ 57) or walk up to the authorized crater zone at 2,920m (9,580ft), a trek of around four hours return. The Ferrovia Circumetnea train (www.circumetnea.it) circles the base of Mount Etna starting from Catania in a very scenic 110km (68-mile ride).

THE BASICS

www.aast-nicolosi.it

 Q4

Via Garibaldi 63, Nicolosi, tel 095 911 505; Mon–Fri 9–2, 4.30–7

Tours from Catania and Taormina

Few

 Cable-car ride to upper station (expensive). 4x4 tours (expensive)

HIGHLIGHTS

● Cable-car ride
● The Etna museum of vulcanology at Nicolosi (▷ 57)
● Local produce: almond pastries, olive oil and wine

TIPS

● If it is foggy or windy, the cable car is replaced by 4x4 minibuses. In bad weather all services are suspended.
● A combined ticket for the cable car and 4x4 tour is €60. The journey takes 2.5 hours (www.funiviaetna.com).

Taormina

Isola Bella beach (left); Chiesa San Giuseppe (middle); the Villa Comunale (right)

THE BASICS

www.gate2taormina.com

🗺 R3

ℹ Palazzo Corvaja, Piazza V Emmanuel, tel 094 223 243; Mon–Sat 8.30–2, 4–7

🍴 A good choice (▷ 60)

🚌 From Catania Airport

🚃 Taormina-Giardini

HIGHLIGHTS

● Teatro Greco (▷ 51)
● Palazzo Corvaja
● Villa Comunale
● Corso Umberto I
● Borgo Medievale
● Piazza del Duomo
● Cable car from Taormina to the beach at Mazzarò

TIP

● Taormina doesn't have any beaches of its own, but there are attractive pebble coves at Mazzarò (▷ 54), which you can reach by cable car or on foot via a steep path. Two other beaches that have bars and restaurants, at Spisone and Letojanni, are a half-hour walk away.

Sicily's best-loved resort is a charming town with a medieval heart, Greek and Roman amphitheatres, palaces, gardens and elegant churches.

They came This resort has attracted the ancient Greeks and Romans, Carthaginians, Saracens, French and Spanish, followed by writers, artistocrats, film stars, royalty—and even a royal mistress. In fact, one of the town's most beautiful public parks, the Villa Comunale, was created by Scots-born Lady Florence Trevelyan in the late 19th century when she was fleeing the scandal of her love affair with the then Prince of Wales, soon to be King Edward VII.

The sights The highlight is the Teatro Greco (Greek amphitheatre, ▷ 51); the smaller Teatro Romano (Roman amphitheatre) is also worth seeing. Borgo Medievale is the clocktower gateway to the medieval part of town. The 14th-century Palazzo Corvaja surrounds an attractive courtyard and is home to the Tourist Office, while the Duomo, fronted by a pretty fountain, dates back to the 13th century.

Walking around Corso Umberto I is the place to see and be seen, especially during the early evening *passeggiata*. It has plenty of shops, bars and restaurants, and is handy for Piazza IX Aprile, a charming square with breathtaking views to the sea. You can also look at the 17th-century Chiesa San Giuseppe, whose facade is embellished with skulls and crossbones.

Taormina has hosted
a theatre since the
third century BC

TOP
25

Taormina:
Teatro Greco

**Standing high above the sea, with
the fiery majesty of Mount Etna as a
backdrop, Taormina's Greek Theatre
couldn't be more perfectly situated.**

Dramatic scenes Taormina has the second-
largest Greek Theatre in Sicily, built in the third
century BC. What remains today came about
400 years later, when the Romans arrived and
completely transformed it from a theatre into a
gladiatorial arena. Over the next two centuries
they added columns and niches to the stage
area and dug a pit to hold the animals and
fighters between performances.

Panorama With a diameter of 109m (358ft),
it doesn't match up in size to Sicily's largest
Greek theatre (▷ 68), but it remains one of the
best-preserved (although the original seats are
no longer there). With its views of snow-capped
Mount Etna, the Calabrian coast and the Bay of
Naxos, it is the most beautifully situated theatre
on the island.

Coming alive The Teatro Greco is open to
visitors daily and you can walk freely around,
puzzling out how the audience entered through
the three-arched gates, before scrambling up
the *cavea* (seating area) and testing its famous
acoustic properties. The theatre is the venue
for a huge variety of arts events from June to
August. With its magnificent setting and superb
acoustics, it is a perfect venue. In June the
theatre hosts the Taormina Film Fest (▷ 59).

THE BASICS

🚩 R3
✉ Via del Teatro Greco,
Taormina
☎ 094 223 220
🕐 Summer daily 9–7;
winter daily 9–4.30
🍴 A good choice in
Taormina (▷ 60)
🚆 Taormina
♿ Few
💶 Expensive

HIGHLIGHTS

● Views of Etna
● Summer performances
during *Taormina Arte*
● The original seating area
● The Roman columns,
niches, *proscenium* (stage)
and *parascenia* (wings)

TIP

● To find out about arts
events at the theatre, look up
the website www.taormina-
arte.com.

More to See

CATANIA

www.comune.catania.it

Sicily's second city has been wiped off the map about seven times by the wrath of Mount Etna, most notably in 1693, after which the rebuilding transformed it into the showcase baroque town it is today (▷ 56). This was thanks largely to the architectural skills of Giovanni Battista Vaccarini. Attractions in the city include the fountain known as the Fontana dell'Elefante, with its smiling elephant carved from Mount Etna's lava, the Teatro Massimo Bellini, one of Europe's grandest opera houses, and the Anfiteatro Romano, built on the site of an earlier Greek theatre and Catania's best-preserved ancient site.

✚ Q5 ✚ Via V. Emanuele, tel 095 742 5573 (free number from within Italy 088 841 042); Mon–Fri 8.15am–9.15pm ⑪ Putia da Aldo (€–€€; ▷ 60) 🚍 From Catania airport, Taormina, Agrigento, Palermo, Siracusa, Enna and Ragusa 🚃 Catania

ETNALAND

www.etnaland.eu

Sicily's top kids' attraction has a dinosaur park, an amusement park and an aqualand with slides, wave machines, helter skelter, waterfalls and flumes. There are also daily shows with entertainers, including clowns and acrobats.

✚ P5 ✉ C. da Agnelleria 95023, Belpasso ☎ 095 989 7101/2 ④ Jun–early Sep daily from 9 (last admission at 4). See website for opening arrangements at other times of year ⑪ A selection of bars in Piazza Verdi (€) 🚍 None (but coach excursions are available from Catania) ♿ Good 💵 Expensive

GIARDINI-NAXOS

Sicily's fastest-growing resort has beautiful sands and clear waters. The area is divided into *spiaggia libera* (the free beach) and various private lidos where you pay for your sunbeds. There's a promenade lined with cafés, bars and restaurants. In the nearby orange and lemon groves, excavations

The remains of Catania's Anfiteatro Romano, watched over by San Biagio church

have found evidence of a settlement dating back to 734BC, the time of the first Greek colony on the island.

🔒 R3 🛈 Via Tysandros 54, tel 0942 51010; Mon–Fri 9–1, 4–7, Sat 9–1. Closed Sat in winter 🍴 Beach cafés and bars, as well as various bars and eateries in town (€–€€) 🚌 From Taormina

GOLE DELL'ALCANTARA

To the west of Taormina runs the lovely gorge of Alcantara, a 19m-deep (64ft) gash in the landscape carved out by the river Alcantara as it makes its way from Monti Nebrodi to the Ionian Sea near Giardini-Naxos. You can explore it via a lift down to the narrowest point, where there's also a waterfall. The water is freezing cold and you'll need protective clothing (you can hire it).

🔒 Q3 🛈 Lift: May–Sep daily 7.30am–8pm; Oct–Apr daily 7.30–7 🍴 Bar and restaurant on upper level (€€) 🚌 None 🛗 Fair 🖐 Inexpensive–Moderate (for lift and protective clothing)

MESSINA

www.comune.messina.it

Despite being repeatedly damaged by earthquakes and badly bombed in World War II, Messina has weathered its 3,000 years relatively well. The Norman Duomo (cathedral) has been painstakingly restored and its campanile houses one of the world's largest astronomical clocks. The clock puts on a show at noon, when a lion's roar is among the sounds heard. The town is also famously the setting of Shakespeare's *Much Ado About Nothing*.

🔒 S1 🛈 Via Calabria, isolato 301 bis, tel 090 672 944; Mon–Thu 8.30–1, 3–5, Fri 8.30–1 🚉 Stazione Centrale, Stazione Marittima

MONTI NEBRODI

www.parcodeinebrodi.it

Just to the north and northwest of Mount Etna, these mountains are the volcano's smaller sisters, though they are much more expansive, covering an area of 70sq km

Boats on the beach at Giardini-Naxos

The Gole dell'Alcantara— definitely worth photographing

(45sq miles). They rise to 1,500m (4,900ft) and have a landscape more varied than the Madonie (▷ 41), with thick woodlands—including Europe's largest remaining beech forest—and upland pasture-land. It's great for nature-spotting, and views of Etna.

✚ M3 🛈 Via Bellini 79, Cesarò, tel 095 773 2061; daily 9–12, 4–6.30. Also Via Latteri, San Fratelli, tel 094 178 9651; daily 9–12, 4–6.30 ♿ None

TAORMINA: MAZZARÒ

The best and closest beach for Taormina, Mazzarò has a couple of pebble beaches and cute coves and grottoes. Of the two beaches, the southernmost is the more crowded but it also has water sports, sunloungers, parasols and showers. The coast is a marine-life sanctuary and the snorkelling is excellent.

✚ R3 🍴 Beach bars and restaurants (€–€€) 🚌 From Taormina ♿ None ❷ There's a *funivia* (cable car) from Via Luigi Pirandello, in Taormina

TINDARI

The fine archaeological site of Tindari is in a picturesque setting on a lonely rock promontory, cos-seted by cypress and olive trees and prickly pear. The coastal views are breathtaking. Originally called Tyndaris, it was founded in 396BC by the Greeks, though much of what remains was built later by the Romans. Main attractions include a late fourth-century BC theatre, two villas, mosaics and the bath complex. Don't miss the Sanctuary of the Black Madonna, which has become a pilgrimage site.

Concerts and classical dramas are staged at Tindari from June to August (starting at around 9pm). For more information, look up the website www.teatrodeiduemari.net or pick up a programme at the entrance or at the Tourist Office in Via Teatro Greco.

✚ Q2 ✉ Capo Tindari ☎ 0941 369023 🕐 Daily 9–one hour before sunset 🍴 Bars and hotel nearby (€) ♿ None ✋ Inexpensive

Mazzarò is the closest beach to Taormina

Walk around Catania

Baroque meets Roman in this lava city, which has a famous opera house, vibrant markets and great shopping.

DISTANCE: 2.5km (1.5 miles)   **ALLOW:** 3 hours

START

PIAZZA DUOMO
✚ Q5

1 Admire the baroque elegance of the Piazza Duomo. The smiling elephant of the Fontana dell'Elefante is carved from Mount Etna's lava and is said to protect Catania from volcanic wrath.

2 Cross over the piazza to the Duomo, named after Catania's patron saint, Agatha. This fine example of the baroque was rebuilt after the 1669 earthquake.

3 Walk across the piazza to Fontana dell'Amenano and down the steps to Piazza A. di Benedetto to Sicily's liveliest fish market, La Pescheria (▷ 58).

4 Return to Piazza Duomo, then walk north and turn right into Via V. Emanuele II and second-left into Via Sant'Agata. Continue to Piazza Scammacca, bear right at Via Sant'Orsola, then turn right into Via G. Perrotta for Teatro Massimo Bellini—one of Europe's grandest opera houses.

END

PIAZZA CARLO ALBERTO
✚ Q5

8 After 200m (219 yards) turn right into Via Pacini, then right into Piazza Carlo Alberto, to browse around the boisterous market Fera o Luni, (▷ 58).

7 Head east on Piazza Stesicoro towards Via A. Manzoni, then turn left into Via Etnea (Catania's showcase avenue, full of shops and cafés) and continue north.

6 From here go north to Via Sant'Elena, turn right into the Via Penninello, then left into Via A. Manzoni and left again into Piazza Stesicoro. On your right is the Anfiteatro Romano, built on the site of an earlier Greek theatre and Catania's best-preserved ancient site.

5 Head east to Piazza V. Bellini, turn left at Via M. Rapisardi, then left into Via A. di Sangiuliano. Cross Via Etnea then take the second-right into Via Crociferi, full of lovely baroque churches and *palazzi*.

Mount Etna Drive

Enjoy superb views on the fertile lower slopes of Etna before climbing lava fields to Rifugio Sapienza, the start point for tours.

DISTANCE: 96km (60 miles) **ALLOW:** 3–4 hours

 START

 END

TAORMINA
✚ R3

NICOLOSI
✚ Q4

❶ Take the A18 *autostrada* south from Taormina and exit at Fiumefreddo. Follow the signs to Etna Nord on the SS120 through the charming town of Piedimonte Etneo to Linguaglossa, the main tourist centre of Etna's north side, which has a beautiful church of lava and sandstone (35km/22 miles).

❻ Back in the car, take the Strada dell'Etna, constructed in 1934, downhill to Nicolosi (21km/13 miles), a ski resort that's home to the Museo Vulcanológico Etneo (Via Cesare Battisti 32, Fri–Wed 9–1, 4–6), where you can learn about Etna's geology and history.

❷ Continue on the Etna Nord route uphill and through Milo to Zafferana Etneo (21km/13 miles), a pleasant hill town 574m (1,883ft) above sea level, famous for its honey and its hordes of weekend walkers who are drawn to the trails on the wooded slopes behind the village.

❺ Crossing the lunar landscape you will take in the Valle de Bove, a huge chasm that stretches 35sq km (over 13.5sq miles) and 900m (2,742ft) deep. It amounts to almost a sixth of the total size of the volcano. At this height you will certainly hear volcanic rumblings and get a whiff of the unforgettable sulphur smell.

❸ From here follow the signs to Rifugio Sapienza (19km/12 miles), passing through increasingly impressive lava fields. Rifugio Sapienza is some 1,400m (4,600ft) below the summit, from where a cable car runs to the upper station (2,500m/8,200ft), then you can take a guided four-wheel-drive tour to the viewing area.

❹ The vehicle climbs the slopes to the Roman Torre del Filósofo, beyond which the southeast active crater of the summit is visible. Explosions and molten lava are common at this height, as the crater dramatically spews smoke.

Shopping

LE COLONNE
This is one of the best places in Sicily for hand-made jewellery. Inspired by antique designs and using old stones, coral and unvarnished precious metals, the store will design and make any piece to your specifications. The owners, Sanny Alvaro and Leila Correnti, learned their craft from their fathers, and have had their work exhibited as far afield as London and New York.
🕀 R3 ✉ Corso Umberto I 164, Taormina ☎ 094 223 680

FERA O LUNI
This market is formally known as the *Fiera di Catania* (Catania Fair), but its more popular Sicilian name, *Fera o Luni*, means Monday Fair, going back to medieval times when it was, by edict, a one-day event. These days it trades from Monday to Saturday, and a very boisterous place it is, too, although it's great for browsing.
🕀 Q5 ✉ Piazza Caro Alberto, Catania 🕐 Mon–Sat dawn–noon

KERAMEION
www.kerameion.com
See the craftsmen at work in this ceramics studio, then buy one of their creations. (It's a steep climb up the steps off the Corso to reach it.)
🕀 R3 ✉ Salita Santippo, Taormina ☎ 094 223 966

PARISI
www.parisitaormina.it
This elegant women's clothes store is the town's best fashion outlet. It stocks big designer names like Versace, Armani, Prada and Dolce e Gabbana.
🕀 R3 ✉ Corso Umberto I, Taormina ☎ 094 262 6133 🕐 Mon–Sat 9.30–8.30, Sun 10–8.30

PASTICCERIA D'AMORE
www.pasticceriadamore.it
La cassata Siciliana (a rich cake with creamy ricotta) is among the specialities of this Taormina *pasticceria*, 'The Pastry Shop of Love'.
🕀 R3 ✉ Via Costantino Patrick 28, Taormina ☎ 094 223 842

PASTICCERIA ETNA
Local pastries, candied oranges, *torroni* and *cannoli*—among many other confections—are an aromatic and visual delight in the shop window of this award-winning *pasticceria*. The backdrop to all this is a beautifully old-fashioned interior and traditional decor. Don't leave without their speciality, *frutta martorana* (marzipan fruits).
🕀 R3 ✉ Corso Umberto I 112, Taormina ☎ 094 224 735

LA PESCHERIA
Probably the most popular fish market in the whole of Sicily, La Pescheria is a wonderfully chaotic affair. Go there for a taste of fresh molluscs or huge sword-fish but, in spite of its name, this is more than just a fish market. You can also find cheeses, herbs and—if you go far enough towards the periphery—clothes and jewellery.
🕀 Q5 ✉ Piazza Alonzo di Benedetto, Catania 🕐 Mon–Sat 5am–11am

SALVATORI VADALÀ
This shop—the best of those selling coral jewellery in this region—offers everything from strings of plain beads to ornate brooches. It also has one of the best locations in Taormina, close by the magnificent Teatro Greco (Greek Theatre).
🕀 R3 ✉ Via Teatro Greco 27, Taormina ☎ 094 223 985

THE PERSONAL TOUCH
Big towns like Catania have branches of the large Italian stores, but for a more personal touch, shop in the smaller towns and villages. You won't find any shopping malls here, but you'll get personal service in friendly, individually owned stores. You'll also come across rural roadside stalls where farmers sell their own fresh produce, which is good value for money.

Entertainment and Activities

CLUB SEPTIMO

A highly popular night-club, this place attracts gilded youth aged anything between 20 and 40-something. It is frequently the venue of major gala nights and fashion shows.

➕ R3 ✉ Via San Pancrazio 50, Taormina 🕐 Jun–Sep daily midnight–5am; off-season Sat midnight–5am

O'SEVEN

Ostensibly an Irish Pub, you may think O'Seven is as close to one as Taormina is to Dublin. Still, it's a cosy place with tables outside and it's beautifully located behind the town's famous clock tower. But you're more likely to hear jazz played than Irish songs.

➕ R3 ✉ Largo Giuseppe La Farina, Taormina 🕐 Daily, round the clock

IL PICCIOLO

www.ilpicciologolf.com
This 18-hole golf course, in the lovely Gole dell' Alcantara—25km (15 miles) from Taormina—offers some challenging play in the verdant surroundings of woodlands and vineyards. It is 650m (2,123ft) above sea level and has spectacular views of Mount Etna. It's best to book, and you will need to carry some proof of your handicap. Golf packages are available.

➕ Q3 ✉ Via Picciolo, Castiglione di Sicilia 🕐 094 298 6252

TAORMINA ARTE

www.taormina-arte.com
As well as its annual productions in May at the Teatro Greco (▷ below), this company performs at a variety of Taormina locations from June to September.

➕ R3 ✉ Corso Umberto I 19, Taormina 🕐 094 221 142 🕐 Jun–Sep

TEATRO GRECO

In Taormina, this is the place to keep your eye on, for its huge variety of performances throughout the summer. Teatro Greco (▷ 51) is remarkable for its acoustics and is a superb venue for concerts, operas, dramas and other entertainment. Among the companies that stage annual productions here are Taormina Arte (▷ above) and Taormina Film Fest (▷ panel), and the

FILM FEST

The Taormina Film Fest is a major showcase for premieres of art-house films from around the world. It is held each June at the Teatro Greco (▷ this page). Only 21 new films are featured and the prize is a Golden Tauro. Many of its winners have gone on to succeed at the Oscars, the Emmys and the Golden Globe Awards. For more information, see the website www.taorminafilmfest.it.

Teatro dei Due Mare (the Theatre of the Two Seas), which is famous for its delivery of Ancient Greek and Roman plays. For a full list of what's on, check with the website www.gotaormina.com.

➕ R3 ✉ Via del Teatro Greco, Taormina 🕐 094 223 220

TEATRO MASSIMO BELLINI

www.teatromassimobellini.it
Named after composer Vincenzo Bellini, who was born in Catania in 1801, the theatre is a venue for all Sicily's major concerts and operas. If you are lucky, you might catch a performance of Bellini's Norma—the opera performed to mark the theatre's inauguration in 1890.

➕ Q5 ✉ Piazza Teatro Massimo, Via Perrotta Giuseppe 12, Catania 🕐 095 730 6111 🕐 Box office Tue–Fri 9.30–12.30, 5–7, Mon, Sat 9.30–12.30

TERTULIA

By day this is a highly popular bookstore. By night it is a café-bar, spilling into the pedestrian street. Occasionally it's also a venue for concerts of various musical styles but, more often, just a comfortable place to enjoy a beer and a snack.

➕ Q5 ✉ Via Michele Rapisardi 1-3, Catania 🕐 0957 123603 🕐 Daily 7pm–1.30am (may close some days in Aug)

Restaurants

PRICES

Prices are approximate, based on a three-course meal for one person.

€€€ over €40
€€ €20–€40
€ under €20

AL DUOMO (€€€)

www.ristorantealduomo.it
Specializing in the cuisine of eastern Sicily, with a simplicity of heart that is reflected in its decor, Al Duomo is beautifully placed near the cathedral and has a terrace overlooking Piazza Duomo.
✚ R3 ✉ Vico Evrie 11, Taormina ☎ 094 262 5656 🕐 Thu–Tue 11am–11.30pm. Closed Nov–Mar

LA BOTTE (€–€€)

www.labotte1972.it
La Botte (the barrel) was founded in 1972 by the grandmother of the present owners. It was then, and still is now, a post-Teatro meeting place, and specializes in *cucina tipica Siciliana* (typical Sicilian cuisine) and pizza. You can eat outside in summer. It's very busy and service can be slow.
✚ R3 ✉ Piazza San Domenico 4, Taormina ☎ 094 224 198 🕐 Daily 11am–11.30pm

CAFFÈ DEL DUOMO (€–€€)

There are plenty of cafés around Catania's main square but this is probably the most charming, with its elegant decor, a lively *tavola calda* (hot table) with tasty snacks, and those coloured fruits made of marzipan.
✚ Q5 ✉ Piazza Duomo 11-13, Catania ☎ 095 715 0556 🕐 Daily dinner

CASA GRUGNO (€€€)

www.casagrugno.it
In a beautiful 16th-century palazzo, chef Andreas Zangerl prepares Sicilian and European meals, with the menu changing dramatically with the season. With one Michelin star, it's generally regarded as the best place to eat in Taormina, but is very expensive.
✚ R3 ✉ Via Santa Maria de' Greci, Taormina ☎ 094 221 208 🕐 Tue–Sat 11am–midnight, Sun 11am–2.30pm

SICILIAN SPECIALITIES

Arancini Rice balls filled with meat ragù, or with ham and cheese, deep-fried
Bucatini Long, hollow pasta, similar to spaghetti
Caciocavallo Firm, stringy cheese, from cows' milk
Cannoli Tubular pastry filled with ricotta, candied fruits, pistachios and chocolate
Cassata Sponge and marzipan, filled with ricotta, decorated with candied fruit
Panelle Chickpea fritters
Sfincione Thickish bread dough topped with softly stewed onions, tomatoes, anchovies, oregano and breadcrumbs

GRANDUCA (€€)

www.granduca-taormina.com
The dining room, terrace and gardens here all have views of the sea and Taormina's Teatro Greco. The restaurant serves pizzas cooked in a wood-fired oven, along with traditional Sicilian food, including a local favourite, *Spaghetti alla Norma*.
✚ R3 ✉ Corso Umberto I 172, Taormina ☎ 094 224 983 🕐 Thu–Tue lunch and dinner

OSTERIA DEL CAMPANILE (€€)

www.osteriadelcampanile.com
This amiable trattoria overlooks the cathedral square and serves fresh, locally sourced food. The speciality is *Braciolettine alla Messinese*, skewered meats and mushrooms, on a bed of vegetables.
✚ S1 ✉ Via Loggia dei Mercanti 9, Messina ☎ 090 711 418 🕐 Daily 11am–11.30pm (closed Sun in Jul and Aug)

PUTIA DA ALDO (€–€€)

Ideal for taking a lunchtime break after a trip around Catania's *Fera o Luni* market (▷ 58), Putia da Aldo is among the best eateries in the area. It specializes in local pasta and seafood dishes in its first-floor grill-house. Credit cards are not accepted.
✚ Q5 ✉ Piazza Sciuti 2, Catania ☎ 095 331 158 🕐 Mon–Sat lunch

Speckled with UNESCO World Heritage Sites, from Ancient Greek to exuberant Sicilian baroque, this area is almost unfairly bequeathed with glorious attractions. It is also known as the 'kitchen garden of Sicily' and is the inspiration for many up-and-coming chefs.

Siracusa and the southeast

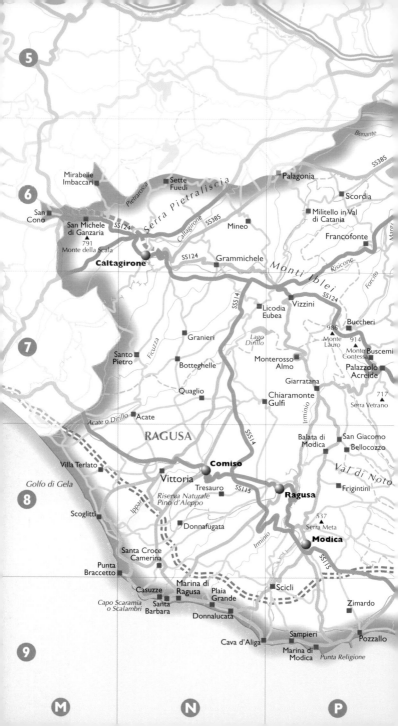

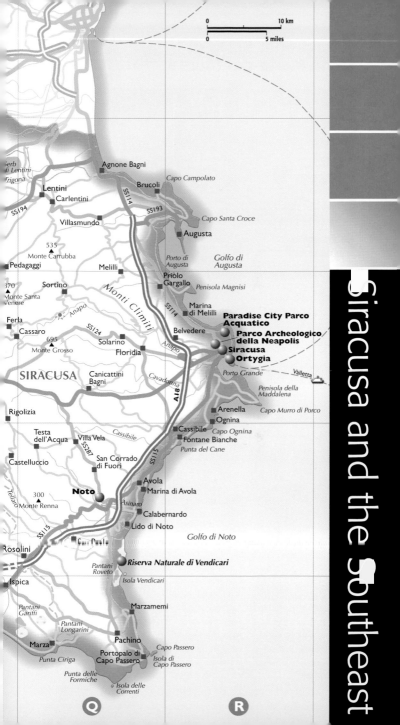

Lentini
Carlentini
SS194
SS194
Villasmundo
535
Monte Carrubba
Pedaggi
Melilli
370
Monte Santa
Venere
Sortino
Monti Climiti
Anapo
Ferla
Cassaro
SS124
695
Monte Grosso
Solarino
Floridia
SIRACUSA
Canicattini
Bagni
Cavadonna
A18
Rigolizia
Testa
dell'Acqua
Villa Vela
Cassibile
Castelluccio
SS287
San Corrado
di Fuori
SS115
Tellaro
300
Monte Renna
Noto
Asinaro
SS115
Rosolini
Cava D'Aleo
Ispica
Pantani
Roveto
Riserva Naturale di Vendicari
Pantani
Gariffi
Isola Vendicari
Pantani
Longarini
Marza
Pachino
Marzamemi
Punta Ciriga
Portopalo di
Capo Passero
Capo Passero
Isola di
Capo Passero
Punta delle
Formiche
Isola delle
Correnti

Agnone Bagni
Brucoli
Capo Campolato
SS114
SS193
Capo Santa Croce
Augusta
Porto di
Augusta
*Golfo di
Augusta*
Priolo
Gargallo
Penisola Magnisi
SS114
Marina
di Melilli
**Paradise City Parco
Acquatico**
Belvedere
**Parco Archeologico
della Neapolis**
Anapo
Siracusa
Ortygia
Porto Grande
Valletta
Penisola della
Maddalena
Arenella
Ognina
Cassibile
Capo Ognina
Fontane Bianche
Punta del Cane
Avola
Marina di Avola
Calabernardo
Lido di Noto
Golfo di Noto
Capo Murro di Porco

Q   **R**

Caltagirone: Scala di Santa Maria del Monte

TOP 25

Flowers decorate the staircase (left and opposite); ceramic tiles on the steps (right)

THE BASICS

www.comune.caltagirone.
ct.it
+ N6
🛈 Via Volta Libertini 3
(upper town), tel 0933
53809; Mon–Fri 9–1, 4–7,
Sat 9–1
🍴 La Scala (€€; ▷ 78)
🚌 From Piazza Armerina
and Enna
🚉 Caltagirone
♿ None

HIGHLIGHTS

● Stunning view from Santa
Maria del Monte church
● Ceramics workshops
● Ponte San Francesco
● Museo della Ceramica (in
Via Roma) for insight into the
local pottery industry

TIPS

● Picnic in the colourful
Giardino della Villa, next to
the Ceramics Museum.
● There's another tourist
office at Galleria Luigi Sturzo,
Piazza Municipio.

This magnificent flight of stairs, decorated from top to bottom with colourful ceramic tiles, is a landmark of the golden sandstone city of Caltagirone.

Stepping out A total of 142 steep steps link Caltagirone's old town, at the top, with the Piazza Municipio, in the new town. Each step is tiled in blue, green, yellow and white, with tiles handcrafted by local ceramicists. No two are the same. The staircase is lined with ceramics workshops, which are a good reason for taking a breather on the way up to the baroque church of Santa Maria del Monte. The steps were built in the 17th century to link the church with Caltagirone's cathedral. A road had been planned, but the incline was too steep. The tiles were not added until 1954. During the festival of *Infiorata* in the last two weeks of May, the steps are carpeted with floral displays. Perhaps most magical is the *Illuminata* festival, on 24 and 25 July, when the steps are lit by thousands of glowing lanterns.

Caltagirone Known as 'Queen of the Hills', Caltagirone is a beautiful city, its churches, palaces and civic buildings lavishly decorated with the ceramic tiles for which it's famed. Via Roma runs into the historic centre, passing over the Ponte San Francesco, an 18th-century viaduct brilliant with majolica decoration. Set on three hills, the area has always been blessed with fine deposits of clay. Arab craftsmen introduced glazing techniques in the ninth century.

Noto

HIGHLIGHTS

● The Duomo's restoration
● Palazzo Nicolaci di Villadorata
● The floodlighting after dark
● Corso Vittorio Emanuele
● Piazza Municipio
● Teatro Comunale

TIPS

● Behind the tourist office is the Villetta d'Ercole—a charming garden of monkey puzzle trees, palms and a fountain of Hercules, which was rescued from Noto Antica.
● Noto Antica, 16km (10 miles) north of Noto, is a quiet and evocative spot with glorious views.

Nicknamed the 'Giardino di Pietra' (Garden of Stone), the honey-coloured *palazzi*, churches and streets of Noto make it the loveliest of all Sicily's baroque towns.

New start The catastrophic earthquake of 1693 razed Noto Antica (Ancient Noto), claiming 1,000 lives and leaving the site on a hilltop on the ridge of Monte Alveria abandoned. The 'new' town was built in the valley below, created by the finest architects of the age.

Perfect perspectives Wide boulevards, expansive piazzas, vistas and stairways all lead the eye from one area to the next, faithful to the 'new' baroque taste for a linear town plan. Over the years the local white limestone has

Clockwise from left: The baroque facade of a town building; detail of an eye-catching carving on a balcony on the Palazzo Nicolaci di Villadorata; the imposing Duomo (San Nicolò cathedral); a row of ornately decorated balconies on the Palazzo Nicolaci di Villadorata

SIRACUSA AND THE SOUTHEAST

mellowed to a honey hue and three of the main streets run east to west, bathing them in sunshine that lends them a peachy-golden glow. The gateway to the main street, Corso Vittorio Emanuele, is the triumphal Porta Reale, built in the 19th century. The majestic Corso runs through three piazzas, passing many of the town's main monuments.

Monuments Dominating the skyline is Noto's immense Duomo, accessed by a flight of steps from the most majestic of the squares, Piazza Municipio. Nearby, the Piazza XVI Maggio is home to the exquisite Teatro Comunale and the soaring convex facade of Gagliardi's Chiesa di San Domenico. The Palazzo Nicolaci di Villadorata, in Via Corrado Nicolaci, is a perfect example of mind-blowing opulence.

THE BASICS

www.comune.noto.sr.it
⊕ Q8
🛈 Piazza XVI Maggio, tel 0931 573779; Mon–Fri 8–2, 3.30–6.30, Sat 9–12, 3.30–6; reduced hours in winter
🍴 Il Barocco (€€; ▷ 78)
🚌 From Siracusa and the coast
🚉 Noto

Duomo
✉ Piazza Municipio
🕓 Daily 9.30–1, 3.30–8

Palazzo Nicolaci di Villadorata
✉ Via Corrado Nicolaci
🕓 Daily 9–1.30, 4–8

Parco Archeologico della Neapolis

The Teatro Greco still hosts performances today

THE BASICS

* R7
* Via Teatro (off intersection of Viale Teocrito and Corso Gelone)
* 0931 66206
* Daily 9–6 (3 in winter)
* Snack bar on site (€)
* From Ortygia: 1, 3, 6, 8, 10, 11,12
* Few
* Expensive

HIGHLIGHTS

* Teatro Greco
* Latomia del Paradiso
* Orecchio di Dionisio
* Roman amphitheatre
* Museo Archeologico Paolo Orsi (▷ 73)
* The flora, including prickly pear cactus, agaves and oleander

TIP

* If you're planning to visit the Museo Archeologico Paolo Orsi, a combined ticket with the Parco Archeologico will save you some euros.

Once a prestigious and wealthy suburb of Siracusa, Neapolis (New Town) was second only to Athens. Now it is an archaeological zone sheltering fantastic Greek and Roman monuments.

Vast area Work began on the classical city in the sixth century BC, using white limestone from the *latomie* (quarries). Today, the area covers around 2.5ha (6 acres) and includes quarries, a Greek theatre and Roman amphitheatre. To the east, about 10 minutes' walk away, the Museo Archeologico Paolo Orsi (▷ 73) traces the history of the pre-Greeks and Greeks in Sicily.

Teatro Greco The plays of Aeschylus, founder of Greek tragedy, were staged here from the fifth century BC. With space for 15,000 spectators, it is one of the world's largest and best-preserved Greek theatres. Of its original 59 rows of seats, 42 rows remain and the acoustics are superb. During Siracusa's Festival of Classical Theatre (May–June), performances are held here at sunset, just as in Greek times.

Paradise and Dionysus Follow the path from the theatre to the Latomia del Paradiso (Paradise Quarry), lined with oleander, citrus fruit, almond and palm trees and speckled with caves. Visit the towering Orecchio di Dionisio (Ear of Dionysus), an ear-shaped cavern where even whispers can be overheard. The Siracusan tyrant Dionysus imprisoned his enemies here and overheard all their conversations.

The Porta Reale (left); resting in Piazza del Duomo (middle); Ragusa Ibla (right)

Tumbling down a hilly ridge, the twin towns of Ragusa Superiore and Ragusa Ibla are a harmonious blend of medieval stepped streets, 18th-century squares and splendid baroque buildings.

Ragusa Superiore Built after the earthquake of 1693, the upper town is laid out on a grid pattern snaking up the side of a hill. Follow the Corso Italia down the hill and the sweep of steps from Santa Maria delle Scale to the more beautiful lower town, Ragusa Ibla.

Ragusa Ibla A labyrinth of cobbled medieval alleys blended with spacious piazzas and handsome baroque buildings of golden limestone make 'Ibla' the jewel of Ragusa. Your eye is immediately drawn to the theatrical Piazza del Duomo, with the Duomo di San Georgio (Wed–Mon 10–1.30, 4–6.30, Tue 4–6.30). This three-tiered 'wedding cake' of a cathedral is a masterpiece of Sicilian baroque. Nearby, the church of San Giuseppe, built in 1590 but badly damaged in the earthquake, has a similarly exuberant facade. Beyond here, the Giardini Iblei (Ibla Gardens; daily 8–8) offer spectacular views across to the valleys.

UNESCO Ragusa is part of the Val di Noto World Heritage Site, which also includes Noto (▷ 66) and Caltagirone (▷ 64). The restoration of previously crumbling *palazzi* and the opening of chic hotels and restaurants are part of the renaissance of this beautiful area.

THE BASICS

www.ragusaturismo.it
🔲 P8
🛈 Via Capitano Bocchieri 33, Ragusa Ibla, tel 0931 221511/529; Tue–Sun 9–2, 4–6
🍴 Duomo (€€€; ▷ 78)
🚌 Buses 1 and 3 commute between upper and lower town. Buses from Modica
🚆 Ragusa (upper town)

HIGHLIGHTS

● Ragusa Ibla
● The local stone
● Baroque architect Rosario Gagliardi's masterpieces, including the Duomo di San Georgio and the church of San Giuseppe
● Views from La Scala di Chiesa di Santa Maria
● Piazza del Duomo
● A stroll in the Giardini Iblei

DID YOU KNOW?

● Most of the island's fruit and vegetables are grown in the province of Ragusa.

Siracusa: Ortygia

TOP 25

HIGHLIGHTS

- Piazza del Duomo
- Il Duomo
- Fonte Aretusa
- Waterfront views
- Galleria Regionale di Palazzo Bellomo
- Sunset lagoon views
- Tempio di Apollo

TIPS

- The island is closed to tourist traffic; leave your car in the car park near the Ponte Umberto.
- Many of the baroque treasures are floodlit at night.
- Ortygia is very fashionable, with wine bars, gourmet restaurants, boutique hotels and elegant shops.

The tiny island of Ortygia is where Siracusa dips its toes into the sea. It's the historic heart of the eighth-century BC city that, according to the Roman orator Cicero, was 'the greatest Greek city'.

Historic island On Sicily's southeastern tip, this teardrop-shaped island is connected to the mainland by a bridge. On it are reminders of more than 2,500 years of history encompassing architectural styles from pagan to Greek, Roman, medieval Norman and Sicilian baroque.

Beautiful baroque At the heart of Ortygia is the Piazza del Duomo, one of Sicily's most beautiful baroque piazzas. The focal point is the Duomo (daily 8–12, 4–7), built on the site of a fifth-century BC Temple of Athena.

A street café in Piazza del Duomo (left); the Fonte Aretusa, a freshwater spring (middle); the beautiful baroque Duomo (right)

Fonte Aretusa South of the cathedral on Ortygia's prettiest stretch of waterfront is the Fountain of Arethusa, the spring that attracted the first settlers. Legend names it after the sea nymph Arethusa, who fled underwater to Siracusa to try to escape the amorous attentions of the river god Alpheus. Nearby, the remains of the Tempio di Apollo (Largo XXV Luglio) date back to the sixth century BC, and are Sicily's oldest Doric temple remains.

Art treasures The Galleria Regionale di Palazzo Bellomo, in Via Capodieci, has re-opened after major restoration. It houses one of Sicily's greatest art collections, with masterpieces including Caravaggio's poignant *Burial of St. Lucy* (1608) and Antonello da Messina's *The Annunciation* (1474).

THE BASICS

www.comune.siracusa.it
+ R7
ℹ Via Maestranza 33, Ortygia, tel 0931 464255; Mon–Sat 8.30–1.45, 4.30–7
🍴 Don Camillo (€€€; ▷ 78)

Galleria Regionale di Palazzo Bellomo
www.regione.sicilia.it/beniculturali/palazzobellomo
✉ Via Capodieci 14
☎ 0931 69511
🕐 Tue–Sat 9–7, Sun 9–1
♿ Moderate

More to See

Siracusa

ACQUARIO, ORTYGIA

This little aquarium, next to the Fonte Aretusa, has displays of colourful fish from the Ionian Sea and more tropical varieties. There's also a good selection of shells.

➕ R7 ✉ Via Picherali, Ortygia ☎ 0931 167 4461 🕐 Daily 10–7 🚌 To Ortygia ♿ Few 💷 Moderate

CATACOMBE DI SAN GIOVANNI

Beneath the ruined church of San Giovanni is a huge labyrinth of tunnels used from Roman times to the sixth century AD for burying the dead. Second only in size to the catacombs in Rome, it is a pilgrimage site as St. Paul is said to have preached here. In this subterranean world, the walls are honeycombed with niches, used as burial places, though the bodies have been removed and buried elsewhere.

➕ R7 ✉ Piazza San Giovanni, Siracusa ☎ 0931 67955 🕐 Daily 9.30–12.30, 2.30–6 🚌 To Archaeological Zone ♿ None 💷 Moderate ❓ Guided tour only

MUSEO ARCHEOLOGICO PAOLO ORSI

www.regione.sicilia.it/beniculturali

Tracing Sicily's history from prehistoric times through Greek and Roman civilizations, this is one of Europe's largest archaeological museums, with 18,000 items on display. Highlights include the marble Adelphia Sarcophagus (from around AD340) and the voluptuous statue *Landolina Venus*. Both were found in Siracusa.

➕ R7 ✉ Viale Teocrito 66, Siracusa ☎ 0931 464022 🕐 Tue–Sat 9–7, Sun 9–1 🚌 To Archaeological Zone ♿ Good 💷 Expensive

PARADISE CITY PARCO ACQUATICO

This huge water park is great for a family day out. It can get very crowded, especially at weekends.

➕ R7 ✉ Località Spalla 1 (3km/2 miles north of Siracusa centre) ☎ 0931 761474 🕐 Mid-Jun to mid-Sep daily 9.30–6.30 🍴 Cafés and restaurants on site (€) 🚌 From Melilli ♿ Good 💷 Expensive

See tropical fish, along with Sicilian underwater creatures, at the Acquario

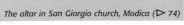

The altar in San Giorgio church, Modica (▷ 74)

The Southeast

COMISO

www.ragusa-sicilia.it/english

For some low-key baroque pleasures, head for Comiso. Rebuilt after the 1693 earthquake, this town is sprinkled with baroque monuments, notably the church Santissima Annunziata (1772–93), with a beautiful blue dome. Overlooking the town is the 15th-century Aragonese castle, built by the powerful Naselli family.

✚ N8 🍴 Bars and restaurants in town (€–€€) 🚇 From Ragusa and Siracusa 🚌 Comiso

MODICA

www.comune.modica.rg.it

Set among limestone hills in the Val di Noto and rebuilt after the 1693 earthquake, this is a lovely town, famous for its baroque architecture and for its chocolate. Modica Alta at the top clings to a rocky spur and a flight of 250 steps leads to the spectacularly flamboyant Chiesa San Giorgio. The church is the work of celebrated baroque architect Rosario Gagliardi and is dedicated to the upper town's patron saint. Down in Modica Bassa, more dizzying steps lead to the lavishly rebuilt Chiesa di San Pietro. You'll see shops advertising *vero cioccolato Modicano* everywhere: Granular and delicious, it is made to 16th-century recipes.

✚ P8 🄴 Corso Umberto I (Modica Bassa), tel 0932 753324; Apr–Sep daily 9–1, 4–8; Oct–Mar daily 9–1, 3.30–7.30 ✉ Churches open daily 9–12, 4–7 🍴 Bars and restaurants in town

RISERVA NATURALE DI VENDICARI

www.parks.it/riserva.oasi.vendicari

The lagoons of this coastal nature reserve attract 200 species of migratory birds and are also home to flamingoes, among other indigenous birds. The area is fringed by soft, white, sandy beaches.

✚ Q8 🄴 Pantano Grande (south of Noto, off SP19 Pachino road), tel 0931 571457; daily 7am–8pm (until 6.30 in winter)

The dome of Chiesa Madre di Santa Maria delle Stelle, in Comiso

A view over Modica

Walk in Ortygia

Stroll around Siracusa's island heart, in the shadow of fine classical monuments, medieval *palazzi* and glorious baroque churches.

DISTANCE: 3.5km (2 miles)   **ALLOW:** 2–3 hours

START

PONTE UMBERTINO
R7

1 Cross the Ponte Umbertino, walk through Piazza Pancali to the Tempio di Apollo (656BC)—the sunken remains of Sicily's oldest city temple, only discovered by chance in 1862.

2 Continue on the Via Savoia on the right of the temple, then walk along to the Porta Marina gateway, overlooking the boats in the Porto Grande.

3 Walk through the gateway and along Via Ruggero Settimo until you spot the trees below you on the right. Turn left up Via Collegio and, at the T-junction, bear right into the lovely Piazza del Duomo (▷ 70–71).

4 Walk to the end of the piazza and go straight down Via Picharale, then right to emerge at the Fonte Aretusa (▷ 70–71). Perhaps enjoy a drink or leisurely meal at one of the waterfront cafés and restaurants.

END

PIAZZA DEL DUOMO
R7

8 Turn right down Via Giudecca, then second-right onto Via del Crocifisso. At the junction, turn left then right to follow Via Minerva, leading you back to Piazza del Duomo.

7 Turn right along Via Maestranza, continuing to the crossroads and the church of the Immacolata.

6 With your back to the Castello, go down Via Salomone, at the junction cross and continue along Via San Martino. At the junction with Via Capodieci bear right, then almost immediately left into Via Roma and continue down to Piazza Archimede, admiring the central fountain depicting Arethusa.

5 From here stroll along the shaded Foro Vittorio Emanuele, enjoying the views. Backtrack to the Fonte Aretusa and continue, hugging the waterside, to the huge Castello Maniace (1239) at the southernmost tip.

Shopping

Siracusa
LE ANTICHE SIRACUSE
This famous café-cum-*pasticceria* has a well-stocked gift shop next door, selling locally crafted ceramics, oils, wines and regional produce.
✚ R7 ✉ Via Maestranza 2, Siracusa ☎ 0931 483003

GALLERIA BELLOMO
www.bellomogallery.com
Around the corner from the Fonte Aretusa, this shop gives an insight into the age-old papyrus industry in Ortygia. Items on sale include papyrus notebooks, cards and paintings.
✚ R7 ✉ Via Capodieci 47, Ortygia, Siracusa ☎ 0931 61340

KENT
In this beautiful shop selling individual and stylish clothes for men and women you'll find both classics and up-to-the-minute designs.
✚ R7 ✉ Via Maestranza 23, Siracusa ☎ 0931 68001

ORTIGIA
The toiletries and candles sold here are made from natural ingredients and are all exquisitely scented and packaged.
✚ R7 ✉ Via Maestranza 12, Siracusa ☎ 0931 461365

The Southeast
ACETI SANDRINE
Choose from a wide selection of men's and women's shoes and other leather goods, at excellent prices.
✚ Q8 ✉ Via Corradino Sinatra 13, Noto ☎ 0931 835677

L'ALIMENTARE SCIMONELLO
Tomatoes grown around this little town are famously sweet and succulent. This grocery shop is the perfect place to stock up on sun-dried tomatoes, chillies, nuts and dried fruit.
✚ Q9 ✉ Piazza Vittorio Emanuele, Pachino ☎ 0931 841772

ANTICA DOLCERIA BONAJUTO
www.bonajuto.it
This is the oldest chocolate-maker in Modica—a town famous for its tradition of Aztec

---

CHOCOLATE

Modica is famous for its chocolate, still made the same way it was in the 16th century, when the Conquistador Spaniards introduced ancient Aztec recipes to Sicily. Made only with pure cocoa and sugar, it is sublimely dark with a grainy, crunchy texture and can be flavoured with cinnamon, chilli, vanilla and orange—all traditional Aztec flavourings. Also known as *cioccolato di vetro* (glass chocolate), one of Modica's best makes is Bonajuto.

---

chocolate. It may be spicy or sweet, but it's always delicious.
✚ P8 ✉ Corso Umberto 159, Modica ☎ 0932 941 2225

ANTICA DROGHERIA
Browse the array of gourmet delicacies, from savoury cheeses, salami and hams to sweet jams, chocolate and honey.
✚ P8 ✉ Via XXV Aprile 57, Ragusa ☎ 0932 652090

BAR GELATERIA COSTANZO
This famous ice-cream parlour (▷ 78) sells delicious *gelati* such as rose and jasmine.
✚ Q8 ✉ Via Spaventa 7, Noto ☎ 0931 835243

BRANCIFORTI
On 'La Scala', this ceramics workshop sells locally crafted beautiful ceramics. Patterns include deep shades of blue with swirling arabesques.
✚ N6 ✉ Scala di Santa Maria del Monte 3, Caltagirone ☎ 0933 24427

PUNTO FORMAGGI E SALUMI
This traditional shop is piled high with all kinds of *salumi* and cheese, as well as freshly made sauces and bottled specialities. It's the best place to track down the deliciously pungent *caciocavallo ragusano*, the local cheese.
✚ P8 ✉ Corso Italia 32, Ragusa ☎ 0932 621694

Entertainment and Activities

Siracusa

LIDO MANIACE

www.lidomaniace.it

This beach area has a platform where you can relax on a sunbed, or you can take a cooling dip in the sea. There are changing facilities, showers and toilets, as well as bars and restaurants.

➕ R7 ✉ Lungomare di Levante, Ortygia, Siracusa
🕔 Summer 💷 Moderate

LA NOTTOLA

www.lanottolaricevimenti.it

This bar is also a jazz club and disco that's popular with a studenty but well-dressed crowd. There is also a pizza restaurant. It's close to Via Maestranza.

➕ R7 ✉ Via Gargallo 61, Siracusa ☎ 0931 60009
🕔 Mon–Thu 8pm–1am, Fri, Sat 8pm–3am

PICCOLO TEATRO DEI PUPI

www.pupari.com

Puppet theatre is a strong tradition in Sicily and this is one of the best places to witness the hand-carved and painted marionettes in action. There is a museum and workshop and performances are given regularly in the summer months.

➕ R7 ✉ Via della Giudecca 17, Siracusa ☎ 0931 465550
🕔 Museum: Mar–Sep daily 10.30–1, 4–7; Oct, Dec daily 11–1, 4–6. Closed Jan, Feb, Nov. Daily puppet performances take place in Aug; see website for show times the rest of the year

LA PISCINA (CALIGOLA)

In summer the focus of this popular disco is the big open-air pool. In winter the three indoor dance floors take centre stage. It's located south of Siracusa in Fontane Bianche.

➕ R7 ✉ Viale dei Lidi, Fontane Bianche, Siracusa
☎ 0931 753633 🕔 Fri, Sat 10pm–3.30am

The Southeast

LA FONTANA VECCHIA

This bar in the lovely town of Noto has a vast terrace that's the place to

---

EASTER CELEBRATIONS

Comiso celebrates Easter Sunday with *La Festa della Pace*. Two different processions set off at 10am, when the statues of Jesus and the Virgin Mary are carried along separate streets until their reunion, at which point the Mother kisses the Son. This is a moment of great rejoicing among the crowds. Similarly, in Modica *La Festa della Vasa Vasa* (Feast of the Kiss), two solemn processions come from different parts of the town, culminating in the meeting of the statues of Jesus and the Virgin Mary at around noon. *'Vasa vasa'* is repeated several times while white doves are released into the sky.

---

be after sunset, when the stones glow honey-gold. The cocktails here are great, as well as the *granite* (ices), which come in a variety of delicious Sicilian flavours, including fresh lemon and *mandorla* (almond).

➕ Q8 ✉ Corso Vittorio Emanuele 150, Noto
☎ 0931 839412 🕔 Apr–Sep daily 7am–midnight; Oct–Mar daily 7am–10pm

HYBLA BIKING

www.hyblabike.com

This company offers guided mountain bike tours, catering for all standards from beginners to experienced. You can also rent mountain bikes here.

➕ P8 ✉ Via del Bagolaro 9, Contrada Fortugnello, Ragusa
☎ 0932 667419

ISTITUTO NAZIONALE DEL DRAMMA ANTICO (INDA)

www.indafondazione.org

The Teatro Greco and Anfiteatro Romano in the Parco Archeologico della Neapolis are the stunning stage sets for superb performances of the classic Greek plays. The highly respected company's innovative approach proves that plays written more than 2,000 years ago still have the power to move the human spirit.

➕ R7 ✉ Parco Archeologico della Neapolis ☎ 800 542 6440 🕔 Performances from May to Jul

Restaurants

PRICES

Prices are approximate, based on a three-course meal for one person.

€€€ over €40
€€ €20–€40
€ under €20

Siracusa

DON CAMILLO (€€€)

www.ristorantedon
camillosiracusa.it

A former monastery is the atmospheric setting for this highly regarded restaurant. The freshest of fish and home-made pasta feature, prepared simply and to perfection with the best of local flavours, all complemented by an excellent wine list.

🔳 R7 ✉ Via Maestranza 96, Ortygia ☎ 0931 67133 🕓 Mon–Sat lunch and dinner

OINOS (€€€)

www.ristoranteoinos.com

Sicilian and Piedmontese specialities are on the menu in this lovely designer restaurant where the white tablecloths match the cool, pale colours of the interior. The cuisine is creative and well-presented by the enthusiastic staff. In summer you can dine on the terrace—a perfect spot for sampling the delicious home-made ice cream.

🔳 R7 ✉ Via della Giudecca 69/75, Ortygia ☎ 0931 464900 🕓 Mon–Sat lunch and dinner. Closed 2 weeks in Feb

The Southeast

BAR GELATERIA COSTANZO (€)

Treat yourself to some of the best ice creams in Sicily. Specialities such as orange, carob and mulberry scented with jasmine are mouthwateringly delicious.

🔳 Q8 ✉ Via Spaventa 7, Noto ☎ 0931 835243 🕓 Daily 11–10

IL BAROCCO (€€)

Pizza and pasta feature alongside fish and seafood in a palatial setting, decorated by the charismatic owner, Graziella. For dining alfresco, reserve a table in the courtyard.

🔳 Q8 ✉ Via Cavour 8, Noto ☎ 0931 835999 🕓 Daily lunch and dinner

DUOMO (€€€)

www.ristoranteduomo.it

'From the Sicilian to the Roman, Arab to French,

GARDEN OF SICILY

Most of Sicily's fruit and vegetables are grown in the province of Ragusa. Plump purple aubergines feature, especially delicious when baked with Parmesan cheese *(melanzane alla parmigiana)*. The area is cloaked with vineyards and almond groves. You'll find some of the island's best *gelaterie* (ice-cream parlours) here, with ice creams flavoured with *mandorle* (almonds) or fruit.

Spanish to English, all influences are here'—so says the Duomo's charismatic Michelin-starred chef, Ciccio Sultano. Creative, adventurous gourmet cuisine is elegantly served and beautifully presented in surroundings to match.

🔳 P8 ✉ Via Capitano Bocchieri 13, Ragusa ☎ 0932 651265 🕓 Tue–Sat lunch and dinner. Closed 10 days in Jan; 10 days in Jul; 19–29 Nov; Sun and Mon lunch May–Sep; Sun evening and Mon in alternate months. Reservations are essential

GELATI DIVINI (€)

www.gelatidivini.it

Divine *granite* (flavoured ices) and ice creams in every flavour imaginable (including wine) make Gelati Divini one of Sicily's most celebrated *gelaterie* (ice-cream parlours). Don't leave Ragusa without trying at least one.

🔳 P8 ✉ Piazza del Duomo 20, Ragusa ☎ 0932 228989 🕓 Daily 9.30am–10pm

LA SCALA (€€)

At the bottom of Caltagirone's famous staircase, this former 18th-century palazzo is the setting for a perennially popular restaurant. Expect traditional Sicilian cuisine and good, regional wine.

🔳 N6 ✉ Scalinata Santa Maria del Monte 8, Caltagirone ☎ 0933 57781 🕓 Thu–Tue lunch and dinner

The Valley of Temples at Agrigento and the stunning Roman mosaics at the Villa Romana are world famous. Less known are the picturesque villages of the interior, where you are never far away from some glorious views and traditions that continue just as they have done for centuries.

The Heartland and the South Coast

1558
Monte
Sambughetti

Lago Ancipa

1013
Monte Schino
della Croce

1242
Serra di Vitto
o di Caginia ▲

Cerami

Troina

SS575

Calogero

SS120
Sperlinga

Nicosia

Gagliano
Castelferrato

Sotto di Troina

Salso

SS121

Carcari

1025
Monte la Guardia

Villadoro

Portella Creta

Nissoria

Agira

Lago Pozzilo

Regalbuto

Salso

Centuripe

825
Monte
Matarazzo

Cacchiamo

Villapriolo

Leonforte

Morello

San Giorgio

ENNA

*Lago
Nicoletti*

Santa Caterina Villarmosa

Calascibetta

Catenanuova

Muglia

Portella
del Vento
Xirbi

A19

Enna

Calderari

Mulinello

487
Cozzo Arginemele

A19

San
Cataldo

Caltanissetta

SS122

Pergusa

Valguarnera

SS117b

889
Monte
Rossomanno

SS288

*Lago di
Ogliastro*

Borgo
Cascino

Olivo

Aidone

SS626

SS560

Roccella

Pietraperzia

Marcato
d'Arrigo

CALTANISSETTA

Borgo
Baccarato

Delia

Barrafranca

460
Monte Sciorino

Braemi

Piazza
Armerina

SS117b

Sommatino

Delia

Riesi

Mazzarino

Ravanusa

595
Monte d Bubonia

Campobello
di Licata

SS626

534
Monte Gricuzzo

*Lago
Disueri*

Frattoria
Ficuzza

Butera

Niscemi

429
Monte
Desusino

*Lago
Comunelli*

SS90

Ponte Olivo

SS115

Manfria

Gela

SS117b

Priolo

Licata

Falconara

Maroglio

Gela

SS115

*Zona umida il
Biviere di Gela*

Golfo di Gela

L M N

Agrigento: Museo Nazionale Archeologico

TOP 25

HIGHLIGHTS

- Attic vases
- Ephebus of Agrigento
- Marble sculptures
- Telamon
- Mosaics in the Hellenistic-Roman quarter
- Sicily's oldest reproduction of the Trinacria, the symbol of Sicily (seventh century BC)
- Marble sarcophagi

TIP

- A combined ticket is available for both the Archaeological Museum and the Valle dei Templi (▷ 84)–a good saving.

Attracting more visitors than any other archaeological museum in Sicily, the statues, artefacts and superb Greek vases displayed here help clothe the bare bones of history shown in Agrigento's excavations.

Orientation This very fine collection is partly housed in the remains of a medieval Cistercian monastery. The first 11 rooms are dedicated to finds from Agrigento itself, representing the full flowering of the great Hellenistic civilizations, while Rooms XII to XVII showcase finds from the entire provinces of Agrigento and Caltanissetta. Across the road from the museum is the Hellenistic-Roman quarter, an ancient residential area with vestiges of villas, taverns and shops, some paved with mosaics.

A giant telamon (human figure) from the Temple of Olympian Zeus (left); a carving on a Greek sarcophagus (middle); the Ephebus of Agrigento statue dates from the fifth century BC (right)

Of vases and marble In Room III are priceless red and black Attic vases dating from the third century BC, including a rare white ground crater (a large bowl used to mix water and wine) dating from 440BC. It depicts Perseus freeing Andromeda. In Room V you find the famous marble statue *Ephebus of Agrigento* (480–470 BC)—an athletic naked 'Adonis', thought to represent a participant at the Olympic Games. Elsewhere, look for the marble statuette of Aphrodite at her bath and the poignant child's marble sarcophagus (second century AD).

Giant among men In Room VI is a recon-structed giant telamon (human figure) that decorated the facade of the Temple of Olympian Zeus (▷ 85). Made of small blocks of tufa, it measures 7.65m (25ft).

THE BASICS

www.parcovalledeitempli.it

➕ J6

✉ Via dei Templi, Contrada San Nicola

☎ 0922 401565

🕐 Tue–Sat 9–7, Sun, Mon 9–1

🍴 Café in museum grounds (€)

♿ Fair

💰 Expensive

DID YOU KNOW?

● In Greek sculpture, Ephebus represents ideal male beauty.

Agrigento: Valle dei Templi

HIGHLIGHTS

● Tempio della Concordia
(Temple of Concord)
● Tempio di Ercole
(Temple of Hercules)
● Tempio di Zeus Olimpico
(Temple of Olympian Zeus)
● Telamon
● Tempio di Castore e
Polluce (Temple of Castor
and Pollux)

TIPS

● The sites are very exposed,
so take a sun hat and plenty
of water.
● Giardino della Kolymbetra
(Kolymbetra Garden) is a
lovely shady spot for a stroll.

**The remains of some of the grandest
temples in the Greek world, strung along
a ridge above the sea, are a reminder of
the transience of wealth and power.**

Wealthy city The Valley of the Temples, a
UNESCO World Heritage Site, reflects the power
that was once Akragas, Sicily's richest city. In
the eastern zone, traversed by the ancient Via
Sacra, the first of the treasures is the Tempio di
Ercole (Temple of Hercules)—the oldest, built in
520BC. Much of it is now in ruins, but eight
columns are visible on the southern side, rebuilt
in 1924–31. Nearby, the honey-gold Temple of
Concord is one of the world's best-preserved
Greek temples. Converted into a Christian
church in the sixth century AD, it was originally
built around 430BC and has 34 Doric columns.

Clockwise from left: This toppled telamon figure was one of 38 that decorated the Temple of Olympian Zeus; the remains of the Temple of Dioscuri; the Temple of Concord, with its 34 Doric columns; the Temple of Hera; visitors shelter from the sun as they walk between the temples

West for Zeus Across the road lies the Western Zone and the ruins of the Tempio di Zeus Olimpico (Temple of Olympian Zeus), once the world's largest Doric temple. At 113m (371ft) long by 36m (118ft) wide, it is larger than a football pitch. The gigantic toppled figure (telamon) that lies on the ground is one of the original 38 that supported the architrave of the temple, like Atlas figures carrying the world on their shoulders. Nearby is the entrance to the Giardino della Kolymbetra, a garden dug out by Carthaginian prisoners but now an archaeological area and an oasis of greenery, agaves and olive trees, studded with ancient stones. West of here you come to the symbol of Agrigento, the Temple of Castor and Pollux, named after the twins born to Zeus. It is a 19th-century reconstruction.

THE BASICS

www.parcovalledeitempli.it

🔼 J6

✉ Piazzale dei Templi, 2km (1.2 miles) from Agrigento

☎ 0922 621611

🕐 Daily 8.30–7 (until dusk in winter; until 10pm in Jul, Aug)

🍴 At entrance, and café near Temple of Concord (€)

🚌 1, 2, 3 from Agrigento train station

♿ Few

💶 Expensive

Piazza Armerina: Villa Romana del Casale

The Villa Romana del Casale is famous for its mosaics

THE BASICS

www.villaromanadelcasale.it
✚ M6
✉ Piazza Armerina
☎ 339 265 7640
🕐 May–Sep daily 8–6; Oct–Apr daily 9–4 (but reduced hours during restoration work)
🍴 Restaurant (€€) and bar (€) outside main entrance
🚌 From Piazza Armerina, Piazza San Marescalchi, May–Sep
♿ Few
💷 Moderate

HIGHLIGHTS

● Salone del Circo (Circus Hall)
● Sala della Piccola Caccia (Room of the Small Hunt)
● Corridoio della Grande Caccia (Corridor of the Great Hunt)
● Sala Ragazze in Bikini (Room of the Bikini Girls)
● Triclinio (Banquet Hall)

The enormous ruins of this magnificent Roman villa boast the finest mosaics in situ anywhere in the Roman world.

Buried treasure Now a UNESCO World Heritage Site, the Villa Romana probably dates from the late third century AD. Its owner was likely to have been a member of the Imperial family. Buried by a mudslide for centuries, it wasn't until treasure was found in 1950 that excavations began in earnest. Each of the 40 rooms is lavishly decorated with mosaics on every floor surface—more than 3,500sq m (37,600sq ft)—the largest group in existence anywhere in the Roman world.

Sensory feast The Salone del Circo (Circus Hall) shows chariot races at Rome's Circus Maximus, while the Frigidarium (cold baths) are decorated by sea nymphs, centaurs and monsters of the deep. The Corridor of the Great Hunt is the mesmerizing focal point of the villa. The mosaic floor seems to come to life in a flurry of chariots, lions, elephants and other wild beasts. In the famous Room of the Bikini Girls, bikini-clad maidens work out with weights, hoops and other paraphernalia that would not be out of place in a modern gym. Nearby, the Great Hall is dominated by the vibrant, often violent mosaic *The Twelve Labours of Hercules*.

Ongoing restoration The perspex roof created sauna-like conditions, harming the mosaics. It is being replaced and the mosaics restored.

More to See

ENNA

www.apt-enna.com

Enna clings to a lofty mountain-side in the island's very heart, 935m (2,844ft) above sea level, and is Europe's highest provincial capital. Fought over by the Greeks, Romans, Arabs and Normans, the great testimony to this turbulent past is the 13th-century Castello di Lombardia, built by Frederick II high on the easternmost spur of Enna's craggy, often cloudy, ridge. On clear days, the views are wonderful.

➕ M5 ℹ️ Via Roma 413, tel 0935 528288; Mon–Sat 9–1, 3.30–6.30 🍴 Centrale (€€; ▷ 92) 🚌 From Catania and Palermo 🚋 Enna ❓ For a walk, ▷ 88

ERACLEA MINOA

Midway between Agrigento and Selinunte, the ruins of the ancient Greek city of Eraclea Minoa stand high on a white sandstone ridge overlooking a long, sandy beach backed by pine trees. The remnants of this sixth-century BC settlement are still largely unexcavated, but the fourth-century BC theatre, perched on the cliff edge, is spectacularly sited and is still used for performances.

➕ G6 ✉️ Eraclea Minoa ☎️ 0922 846005 🕐 Daily 9–one hour before dusk 🚌 From Agrigento and Sciacca (fairly regular Jun–Sep) ♿ Few 🎫 Inexpensive

SCIACCA

www.comune.sciacca.ag.it

This spa town and vibrant fishing port has a low-key Mediterranean charm. Walls enclose the upper town and through the Porta San Salvatore you walk down the Corso Vittorio Emanuele to the lovely Piazza Scandaliato—perfect for enjoying bay views. The town is noted for its ceramics and for one of the best carnivals in Sicily, with spectacular handmade floats.

✉️ G5 ℹ️ Corso Vittorio Emanuele 84, tel 0925 84121/22744; Mon–Sat 8–2, 4–6 🍴 Bars and restaurants (€–€€) 🚌 From Agrigento and Trapani 🚋 Sciacca ❓ *Carnevale* celebrations take place the week before Ash Wednesday

Fishing boats moored in the harbour at Sciacca

Walk in Enna

Beautiful views abound in this town at the heart of Italy, which clings to the top of a mountain spur.

DISTANCE: 3km (2 miles)   **ALLOW:** 2 hours

START

PIAZZA SAN CATALDO
✚ M5

① With your back to the church of San Cataldo, walk diagonally across Piazza Cataldo, then up Via Roma into Piazza Vittorio Emanuele.

② Continue up Via Roma, Enna's main street, passing San Marco on the left and Piazza Umberto I on your right—one of the string of piazzas that punctuate Via Roma's uphill course. Walk on up until you see Piazza Colaianni on your right.

③ Via Roma now leads up to the 14th-century Duomo, topped with an elegant campanile. The handsomely restored baroque interior is a visual treat. Look for the columns decorated with grotesques, including snakes with human heads.

④ From here walk through Piazza Mazzini. Where the street narrows, you are in Via Lombardia, which ends in a flourish in the spacious piazza in front of the massive fortress, the Castello di Lombardia (▷ 87).

END

PIAZZA VITTORIO EMANUELE
✚ M5

⑦ Leave the piazza in the northwest corner and head down Viale Marconi to the gardens near Piazza Crispi, which have probably Enna's most stupendous viewpoint. Then cut through and back to Piazza Vittorio Emanuele.

⑥ Retrace your steps to the front of the Castello and take the Viale Caterina Savoia on the right, glimpsing spectacular views downhill through the trees. Continue down past the post office on your right, to emerge at Piazza Garibaldi.

⑤ Follow the left-hand road around the castle, past the entrance steps, then continue straight on until the rocky mass of the Rocca di Cerere looms into view. This is one of Sicily's most ancient holy sites, named after Ceres, the Roman earth-mother goddess. In the fourth century BC it was the site of a magnificent temple.

Shopping

ABBAZIA DI SANTO SPIRITO

This abbey church, attached to Agrigento's Museo Civico, is famous for its delectable almond sweets, which are still made by the Benedictine nuns based here. Also delicious is the celebrated *cuscusu*—a semolina pudding mixed with pistachio nuts and chocolate. To purchase the exquisite confectionery, ring the bell marked *monastero* on the right of the cloisters.

✠ J6 ✉ Via Santo Spirito, Agrigento ☎ 0922 590371

CARLINO ANTONINO

www.carlinoceramiche.it
A member of the Associazione Ceramisti di Sciacca, this shop specializes in figurines. These depict uniformed figures from the 18th century to the present day. The store also sells plates.

✠ G5 ✉ Corso Vittorio Emanuele 46, Sciacca ☎ 0925 26513

FORMAGGI DI DIO

This cheese lover's haven is piled high with local specialities, such as pungent *Piacentu* (with saffron and black peppercorns). It also specializes in a variety of wines, olive oils and cured meats and so is an ideal place to stock up for a picnic.

✠ M5 ✉ Via Mercato Sant'Antonio 34, Enna ☎ 0935 25758

GASPARE CASCIO

Famous for its ceramics, Sciacca is a treasure trove of craft shops. This little store is abundant in everything from platters and bowls to little ornaments, decorated in the signature deep blue, turquoise and yellow hues. Prices are reasonable, too.

✠ G5 ✉ Corso Vittorio Emanuele 115, Sciacca ☎ 0925 82829

OPEN SPACE

Part of a large interior-decorations store in Enna, this shop has a wide choice of ornamental

---

SYMBOL OF SICILY

When the Greeks discovered Sicily in the eighth and seventh century BC they called it Trinacria (the land with three points). Today, the island's symbol is depicted by three legs with a face in the centre, originally that of Medusa, but now one with a softer look. The hill town of Enna marked the crossroads of ancient Sicily's three provinces and in this region you will find plenty of souvenir tiles, plates and jewellery decorated with the Trinacria symbol. Look, too, for models of traditional colourful carts, which were once the island's major form of transport. Carts are still used in Sicily on feast days and at funerals.

---

and practical gifts for the home, as well as a good selection of ceramics.

✠ M5 ✉ Via Roma 300, Enna ☎ 0935 504701

PASTICCERIA IL DOLCE

Indulge your tastebuds in one of Sicily's best pastry shops. Delicious *cannoli* oozing with sweet ricotta, almond biscuits and many other kinds of mouthwatering sweet pastries are displayed to tempt you.

✠ M5 ✉ Piazza Sant'Agostino 40, Enna ☎ 0935 24018

POLLINI

www.pollini.com
Beautiful shoes, accessories and handbags are all on display in this designer shop in Agrigento. All are handmade and the superb craftsmanship shines through these exquisite leather creations.

✠ J6 ✉ Via Atenea 147, Agrigento ☎ 0922 20170

RUSSO FERNANDO

This upmarket shop in Enna prides itself on traditional regional specialities. There's a huge array of cheeses and Sicilian liqueurs to choose from, such as Ficodi, flavoured with prickly pears, and *digestivi*, subtly spiced with citrus and cinnamon.

✠ M5 ✉ Via Mercato Sant'Antonio 16, Enna ☎ 0935 501031

Entertainment and Activities

AUTODROMO DI PERGUSA

www.autodromopergusa.it
Near Enna, the Lago di Pergusa is the stunning lakeside location of the circuit where regular Formula 3 and Formula 3000 motor racing and motor bike races take place. The circuit encircles Pergusa Lake—Sicily's only natural lake. In summer it is the setting for sailing competitions.
✚ M5 ✉ Via Nazionale 10, Pergusa ☎ 0935 541661 (9km/5 miles south of Enna)

BAR CHARLIE

The area around Sciacca's harbour has plenty of restaurants and bars—it's a great place to drink in the views. This popular bar is ideal for supping a long cool beer and maybe enjoying a snack. Credit cards are not accepted.
✚ G5 ✉ Piazza Dogana 12, Sciacca ☎ 0925 21239
🕔 Mon–Fri 6am–midnight, Sat 6am–12.30am

CENTRO IPPICO CONCORDIA

www.provincia.agrigento.it
This is a well-managed riding school with 20 horses.
✚ J6 ✉ Viale Cavalieri Magazzeni 44, Agrigento ☎ 0922 412903

ENOTECA SPIZZULIO

You'll find a great choice of wines in this cosy *enoteca* (wine bar) where you can also nibble on cheese, olives and plates of cold meat. If you're feeling hungry, more substantial appetites are also well catered for in the adjoining restaurant.
✚ J6 ✉ Via Panoramica dei Templi 23, Agrigento ☎ 0922 20712
🕔 Mon–Sat 7pm–11pm

ERACLEA MINOA PERFORMANCES

Perched high on a ridge overlooking the sea, this ancient Greek site is the spectacular location for classical drama and concerts in summer.
✚ G6 ✉ Eraclea Minoa ☎ 0922 846005 🕔 Jul–Aug evenings

NOBEL-PRIZE WINNER

Luigi Pirandello was born just outside Agrigento in 1867. A famous playwright, he was obsessed with the illusory nature of existence and the isolation of man, foreshadowing the works of Samuel Becket and Harold Pinter. He achieved fame with his play *Six Characters in Search of an Author* (1921) and was awarded the Nobel Prize for Literature in 1934. His works are often staged during Agrigento's summer drama festival and his birthplace is now a museum, Casa Natale di Luigi Pirandello (past the Valle dei Templi, Contrada Caos, tel 0922 511826; daily 9–12, 3–7; inexpensive).

MOJO WINE BAR

Relax to some good jazz sounds while enjoying a glass or two of Sicilian wine, accompanied, perhaps, by cold cuts of meat and cheese. This spot attracts a stylish crowd, who come also for the setting in an attractive piazza.
✚ J6 ✉ Piazza San Francesco 11-13, Agrigento ☎ 0922 463013
🕔 Mon–Sat until 11pm

MUNICIPIO TEATRO COMUNALE LUIGI PIRANDELLO

Named in honour of Nobel-Prize winner Pirandello (▷ panel), this theatre runs plays from October to April.
✚ J6 ✉ Piazza Luigi Pirandello, Agrigento ☎ 0922 590271

PISCINA COMUNALE

If you're wilting in inland Enna's heat, this outdoor swimming pool is a great way of cooling off in summer.
✚ M5 ✉ Piazzale Onesti, Pergusa (Enna) ☎ 0935 531123 🕔 Summer only

VALLE DEI TEMPLI CONCERTS

www.agrigentonatura.it
Agrigento's Valley of the Temples is the spectacular backdrop to evening open-air concerts in the summer.
✚ J6 ✉ Piana San Gregorio, Agrigento ☎ 0922 401129 🕔 Aug–Sep

Restaurants

AL FOGHER (€€€)

www.alfogher.net
One of Sicily's most famous restaurants is in a very pleasingly rustic setting. Traditional, local ingredients are served in exciting combinations with a modern twist, such as red mullet encased in a pistachio crust. The service and wine list are exemplary. This gastronomic temple is part of the Slow Food movement. Be sure to book ahead.
✚ M6 ✉ Strada Statale 117 bis, Contrada Bellia, Piazza Armerina ☎ 0935 684123 ⏰ Tue–Sat lunch and dinner, Sun lunch. Closed 1 week in Jan and 20 days in Jul

CAFFÈ MARRO (€)

Enjoy a *gelato* (ice cream) or a mouth-watering hazelnut pastry with your coffee at this elegant, historic café, recently re-opened, which overlooks Enna's two main squares. In summer there's a lovely terrace for alfresco supping and people-watching.
✚ M5 ✉ Piazza Vittorio Emanuele 22, Enna ☎ 0935 591184 ⏰ Daily 8am–10pm

CENTRALE (€€)

www.ristorantecentrale.net
This family-run restaurant has been in business for more than 100 years and is famous for its antipasto buffet. Start your meal with a selection of more than 20 dishes, then feast on freshly made pasta, followed by meat as your *secondo*. Vegetarians are well catered for.
✚ M5 ✉ Piazza VI Dicembre 9, Enna ☎ 0935 500963 ⏰ Sun–Fri lunch and dinner (also Sat Jun–Sep)

HOSTARIA DEL VICOLO (€€–€€€)

www.hostariadelvicolo.it
A warm welcome awaits in this restaurant in the heart of Sciacca's historic centre. It is known for its fusion of Sicilian ingredients with a lighter, 21st-century spin—perhaps treat yourself to the tasting menu. The excellent food

BOOK AHEAD

From the remote interior to the major tourist circuit around Agrigento's Valley of the Temples, good restaurants are much in demand and it isn't uncommon to see queues in the high season. For that reason, it is usually a good idea to book. Nowadays this can be done online as well as by phone or in person, as so many restaurants have websites. Or you can ask your hotel to book on your behalf.

is complemented with a very good wine list.
✚ G5 ✉ Vicolo Sammaritano 10, Sciacca ☎ 0925 23071 ⏰ Tue–Sun lunch and dinner. Closed 2 weeks in Nov

PASTICCERIA GELATERIA DI CATALANO (€)

Delicious ice creams, Sicilian cakes, biscuits and sweets are temptingly displayed in this café/ice-cream parlour.
✚ M6 ✉ Piazza Garibaldi 16, Piazza Armerina ☎ 0935 680167 ⏰ Tue–Sun 9am–8pm

TRATTORIA DEI TEMPLI (€€)

www.trattoriadeitempli.it
Fish and seafood are the specialities here, imaginatively prepared and presented. Vaulted ceilings and terracotta floors complement the dining experience.
✚ J6 ✉ Via Panoramica dei Templi 15, Agrigento ☎ 0922 403110 ⏰ Daily lunch and dinner. Closed Sun Jul–Aug and Fri in alternate months

TRATTORIA LA RUOTA (€€)

www.trattorialaruota.it
Near the Villa Romana, this restaurant specializes in inland Sicilian cooking. Expect home-made pasta and local dishes such as veal and rabbit.
✚ M6 ✉ Contrada Paratore Casale, Piazza Armerina ☎ 0935 680542 ⏰ Daily lunch

Western Sicily

From the fairy-tale medieval mountain town of Erice to coastal neighbours like Marsala and the island of Mozia, the far-western corner of Sicily has many beautiful attractions.

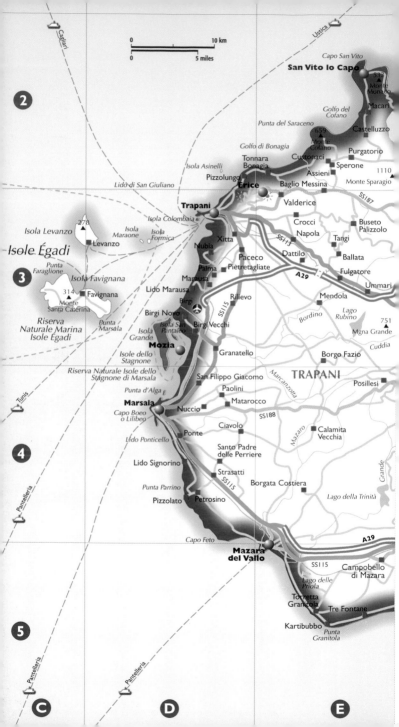

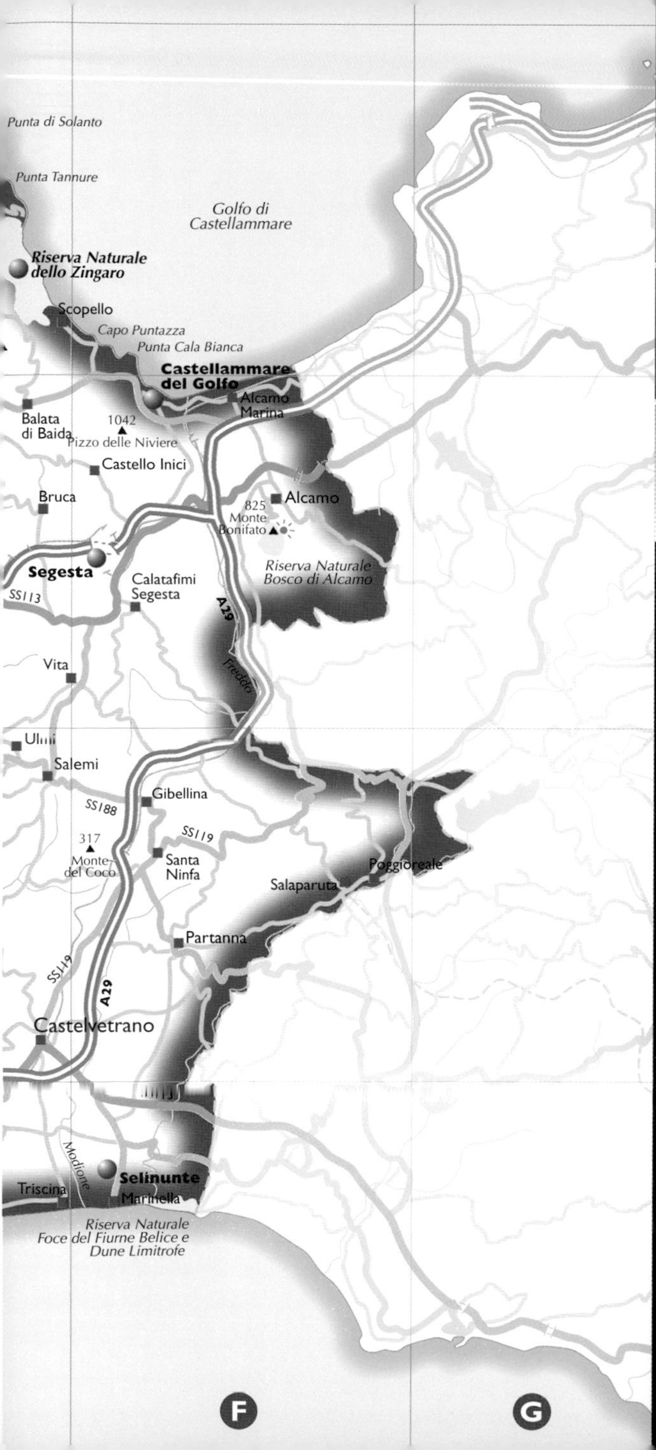

Punta di Solanto

Punta Tannure

Golfo di
Castellammare

Riserva Naturale
dello Zingaro

Scopello

Capo Puntazza
Punta Cala Bianca

**Castellammare
del Golfo**

Alcamo
Marina

Balata
di Baida

1042
▲
Pizzo delle Niviere

Castello Inici

Bruca

825
Monte
Bonifato ▲

Alcamo

Riserva Naturale
Bosco di Alcamo

Segesta

Calatafimi
Segesta

SS113

A29

Trottola

Vita

Ulmi

Salemi

Gibellina

SS188

SS119

317
▲
Monte
del Coco

Santa
Ninfa

Salaparuta

Poggioreale

Partanna

SS119

A29

Castelvetrano

Modione

Triscina

Selinunte

Marinella

Riserva Naturale
Foce del Fiume Belice e
Dune Limitrofe

F

G

Erice

The Castello di Venere (left); a ceramic street light (middle); a place to rest (right)

THE BASICS

www.prolocovalderice.it
🔲 E3
ℹ️ Via Tommaso Guarrasi
1, tel 0923 869388;
Mon–Sat 8–2
🍴 Pasticceria Grammatico
(▷ 104, 106) and many
bars and restaurants
🚌 21 or 23 from Trapani.
Also *funivia* (cable car)

HIGHLIGHTS

● Views on a clear day
● The Giardino del Balio and
its fountain statue of Venus
● Castello di Venere
● The cafés and bars of
Piazza Umberto I
● Mura Elimo Puniche, the
wall constructed more than
2,800 years ago

TIP

● Erice becomes enveloped
in mist at certain times—
very atmospheric, but best
avoided if you're looking for
beautiful views.

**The medieval town of Erice is perched
743m (2,438ft) above the far-western
coast, with superb views of Etna to the
east and Tunisia to the southwest.**

The days of love Erice was founded 3,000
years ago as a shrine to Venus but established
its identity in medieval times. It presents the
perfect image of a walled town with cobbled
streets, grotto-like alleys, flower-strewn
balconies and baroque courtyards. Where the
Temple of Venus once stood, there is now
the 12th-century Castello di Venere, which
incorporates parts of the original site. Given its
associations with the goddess of love, the town
is a popular wedding venue.

Gateway to the past The main entrance to
the town is the Norman Gate, the Porta Trapani,
which leads to Chiesa Madre, a 14th-century
church, later fortified. Its splendid gothic facade
belies the 19th-century interior, though it has
several baroque altars and some 17th-century
paintings. Erice's main square, the Piazza
Umberto I, is home to the Museo Comunale
Cordici, whose collection includes a small fifth-
century BC head of Venus.

Sweet memories The town is littered with
quaint shops and eateries, but there's none
quite so charming as Maria Grammatico's
Pasticceria Grammatico (▷ 104, 106). As well
as selling pastries, it's also a café—and a delightful part of Erice's not-too-distant past.

A fountain (left); walking through an archway (middle); an old wine press (right)

Marsala

The wine of Marsala is world renowned and represents the very 'taste' of Sicily, but the town also has a crucial place in the island's—and Italy's—history.

Historical crossroads When Garibaldi landed with his famous 'thousand' army to begin the War of Italian Unification in 1860, Marsala's place in modern history books was assured. But the town was already celebrated for its wine (▷ 106). The town's story begins in 396BC, when the Phoenicians were forced out of the nearby island of Mozia (▷ 99). The Romans took over after the First Punic War in 241BC and remained until the fall of the Empire, when the Vandals moved in. The town got its present name when the Arabs came in AD830, calling it Marsah-al-Allah ('port of God').

Historic centre Sicily's most westerly town has a historical core dotted with trees and archaeological sites. Piazza della Repubblica is reached through Porta Nuova, a monumental Renaissance gate in the Western wall. Here you find the Chiesa Madre, Marsala's largest church, originally Norman and dedicated to St. Thomas à Becket, Marsala's patron saint. Since the 11th century, the church has been extensively rebuilt. Near the church is the Museo degli Arazzi Fiammingi (Via Giuseppe Garaffa 57), with some wonderful tapestries. See an exhibition on Garibaldi at the Complesso San Pietro, in Via XI Maggio, and a warship from the Punic Wars at the Museo Archeologico, on the seafront.

THE BASICS

www.lagunablu.org
🔶 D4
ℹ Via XI Maggio 100, tel 0923 714097/ 993270; Mon–Sat 8–8, Sun 9–12
🍴 Trattoria Garibaldi (€€; ▷ 106)
🚌 From Trapani
🚊 Marsala

HIGHLIGHTS

● Museo degli Arazzi Fiammingi's 16th-century tapestries of the Holy Wars
● The Complesso San Pietro's permanent exhibitions on Garibaldi (admission free)
● The Phoenician galley wreck at the Museo Archeologico

TIP

● Get a taste of Marsala at Cantine Florio (Via Vincenzo Florio 1) or any other winery where Marsala wine is made.

Mazara del Vallo

TOP 25

A fishing boat (left); inside the Duomo (middle); Collegio dei Gesuiti entrance (right)

THE BASICS

E5

Piazza San Veneranda 2, tel 0923 941727; Mon–Sat 8–2, Sun 9–12

La Bettola dal 1972 (€€; ▷ 106)

From Marsala and Trapani

Mazara del Vallo

HIGHLIGHTS

● Casbah
● The floodlit Norman Castello
● Duomo
● Piazza della Repubblica
● Museo del Satiro Danzante
● Strolling on the *lungomare* (waterfront)

The most important of Sicily's Moorish towns, Mazara boasts the island's largest fishing fleet and a fascinating, labyrinthine old town.

Moorish links Originally a trading post founded by the Phoenicians in the ninth century BC, Mazara later became one of the wealthiest cities in Arab Sicily. Today, you can wander through the exotic maze of souk-like streets of the Casbah (Tunisian quarter).

Historic centre Behind the palm-lined waterfront, the ruins of the Norman Castello and its piazza are the focal point at *passeggiata* time and are splendidly floodlit after dark. Nearby, the imposing Duomo, dating from the 11th century, had an exuberant baroque makeover in the 17th century.

Tall tale In 1998 a local fisherman was amazed to find a bronze leg in his trawling net in the waters between Mazaro and Pantelleria. Weeks later, he and his friends recovered the head and torso of what is now known as *Il Satiro Danzante* (The Dancing Satyr), thought to date back to the fourth century BC. The remains of the satyr, 3m (10ft) tall, are remarkably well-preserved and show him mid-leap, head thrown back ecstatically, dancing. The full story of the fishermen's extraordinary find and the restoration is documented in an excellent video in the Museo del Satiro Danzante, in Piazza Plebiscito (Tue–Sat 9–7, Sun 9–1).

Mozia: Museo Whitaker

Windmills on the salt pans (left); the museum (middle); Il Giovinetto di Mozia (right)

This museum unfolds the secrets of 3,000 years of history. It sits on an island that was once Italy's busiest trading post and Sicily's most powerful city.

Treasure trove Nestling on a lonely island in a lagoon 8km (5 miles) along the coast from Marsala, the Whitaker Museum of Mozia stands on the world's best-preserved Phoenician site and has some of Sicily's most valuable Greek statues. Mozia was home to a colony of Phoenicians from the eighth century BC until they fled to Marsala in 396BC (▷ 97). The large collection includes pottery, jewellery, glassware, stelae (grave markers) and tiny braziers used for burning. The jewellery includes brooches, pendants and collars in gold and bronze. The museum's crowning glory, however, is the life-sized fifth-century BC marble statue *Il Giovinetto di Mozia* (the young man of Mozia).

The idyll At first glance the island of Mozia appears to a rustic idyll whose grounds and surrounding waters are a haven for all manner of intriguing vegetation, wildlife and sea creatures. With its spectacular white salt pans, windmills and aloe-lined footpaths, Mozia appears to float among the tiny islands in the Stagnone wetlands reserve. For centuries it lay in insignificance until 1913, when James 'Pip' Whitaker (1850–1936), an amateur archaeologist and Marsala wine dealer, rediscovered it and excavated the site. He also built the villa that now houses the collection.

THE BASICS

✚ D3
✉ Mozia
☎ 0923 712598
🕐 Apr–Oct daily 9.30–1.30, 2.30–6.30; Nov–Mar 9.30–3
🍴 Restaurant and bar on island, summer only (€€)
🚌 From Piazza del Popolo in Marsala to the ferry (Mon–Sat 8–6, every 60–90 mins; journey time 30 mins)
🚢 Mozia
⛴ Frequent sailings by local fishermen
♿ Ferry poor, island poor, museum good
✋ Museum expensive

HIGHLIGHTS

● The smiling mask representing the demon-god Bes
● The collection of bronze arrows and javelin heads
● The Casa dei Mosaci
● The necropolis dedicated to the goddess Tanit
● Submerged Phoenician causeway that allowed horses and carts to seemingly glide across the water

Riserva Naturale dello Zingaro

TOP **25**

The nature reserve has hidden beaches and an abundance of wild flowers

THE BASICS

www.riservazingaro.it

✚ E2

ℹ Via Segesta 197, Castellammare del Golfo, tel 0924 35108; summer daily 7am–8pm; winter daily 8–4

🍴 None within the park, but bars and restaurants at Castellammare del Golfo and Torre dell'Impiso

🚌 Shuttle buses from Castellammare del Golfo train station

♿ Access on foot only

💰 Inexpensive

HIGHLIGHTS

● For divers, exploring the wrecks and underwater grottos (▷ 105)
● The Capreria, Marinella and Uzzo coves
● The subtropical vegetation, including dwarf fan palms

TIP

● Take food and water as there are no supplies within the reserve.

Sicily's first nature reserve stretches over 7km (4 miles) of unspoilt coastline, with secluded coves and beaches. It is backed by hills rich in rare flora and wildlife.

Gypsy path The name of the park translates as the Gypsy (Romany/Traveller) Nature Reserve and, in all, it occupies some 1,650ha (4,075 acres). At the coastline, spectacularly steep slopes plunge down to a parade of idyllic coves, tiny bays and beautifully clear turquoise water. These can be reached via the reserve's main track, which follows the coastline, and the coves along the path offer superb bathing and snorkelling. Other paths radiate through the hills, with Monte Speziale the highest point at 913m (2,290ft). Along the way there are various shelters and three museums. Inhabitants of the skies include eagles, peregrine falcons and rock partridges. Among the rocks and gorse are rabbits, weasels and hedgehogs. Foxes are there, too, but visible only after dusk, as are nocturnal porcupines, who leave their white needles as calling cards.

Mafia connection Established in 1981, the reserve arose out of a government crackdown on drug-smuggling by the Mafia, who used the well-hidden coves as bases. A planned coastline road, which was part of the crackdown, led to widespread howls of protest and the issue was resolved by turning the whole area into Sicily's first nature reserve. There's still no road, but the coves are no longer so well-hidden.

The Doric temple (left); a wonderful view from the amphitheatre (right)

Sicily's most evocative monument is one of the world's most perfectly preserved survivors of antiquity, standing on a hill in proud isolation.

From Egesta to Segesta The magnificent Doric temple has been here so long that the local wildlife treats it like home, nesting in its crannies and scurrying over its floor. In 1200BC the Segesta site (then called Egesta) became the main city of the Elymi (or Elyminan people), legendary survivors of the Trojan War, who also founded Erice (▷ 96). By the mid-fifth century BC they had become thoroughly Hellenized and the temple, erected between 426 and 416BC, was undoubtedly the work of a great Athenian architect.

Unfinished story As you stand below, this beautiful golden masterpiece looks complete, its 36 columns, entablature and pediment enclosing a space minus a roof. Climb up, though, and you'll see how unfinished the building is—the columns lack the typical Doric fluting, the roof was never built and the stone bosses on the stairs, used to manhandle the stone onto the site, remain in place. No one knows why work did not finish.

Vanishing legacy As well as the nearby classical amphitheatre (▷ 105), the site has crumbled ruins of a mosque, a small church and a Norman castle, all of which testify to Segesta's survival into the Middle Ages.

THE BASICS

🔲 F3
✉ Via Segesta (nearest town is Calatafimi)
☎ 0924 955841
🕐 Daily 9–one hour before sunset (ticket office closes at 6)
🍴 Snack bar on site (€)
🚌 From Trapani; from Castellammare del Golfo in summer
🚃 From Trapani to Segesta-Tempio, then 20-minute walk uphill
♿ None
💶 Expensive

HIGHLIGHTS

● The splendid views
● The interior of the temple at sundown, when the columns glow like gold

TIP

● In summer in odd-numbered years, you can see a play at the amphitheatre (▷ 105). A shuttle bus runs from the ticket office.

Selinunte

TOP
25

The remains of Temple D (left); and Temple E, the most complete structure (right)

THE BASICS

www.selinunte.net

➕ F5

✉ Marinella di Selinunte

☎ 0924 46277

🕐 Daily 9–one hour before sunset

🍴 Pierrot (€€),
Via Marco Polo 108,
Marinella di Selinunte
(daily lunch and dinner).
There is also a bar at the site
entrance (€)

🚌 From Castelvetrano

♿ Visitor centre good,
site poor

💰 Expensive

HIGHLIGHTS

● The Acropolis
● Temple E
● Views of Marinella di
Selinunte and its beach

TIP

● You can hire an electric
cart to take you around the
whole site or just part of it.

The once-mighty Greek city of Selinunte, whose walls guarded a great citadel, temples and a market place, is today a fascinating archaeological jigsaw.

'A great heap' Though some of the pieces are now in place, Selinunte was certainly a jigsaw puzzle to the French author Guy de Maupassant who, in 1885, called it 'an immense heap of fallen columns, now aligned and placed side by side on the ground like dead soldiers'. Earlier in the 19th century, an English team of archaeologists started the first attempts to put it together.

Temples The site is strewn with temples, an acropolis (citadel) and *agora* (market place). Most remarkable are the ruins of three temples to the east of the site, named prosaically as E, F and G. The most complete is Temple E, a Doric building dating to the fifth century BC and probably dedicated to Aphrodite. It was reconstructed in 1958. To the west via a long track are the Acropolis and West Temples (A, B, C, D and O). Temple C is the site's earliest and best-preserved ruin. Its glorious frieze panels are now in the Archaeological Museum of Palermo (▷ 28), but 14 columns have been rebuilt.

Neglect and rediscovery The city got its name from the wild celery (*selinon* in Greek) that grew in abundance on the high plains. Since its destruction by the Carthaginians more than 2,000 years ago, the site was utterly neglected until its 19th-century excavations.

More to See

CASTELLAMMARE DEL GOLFO

www.castellammaredelgolfo.com

The ancient harbour here once served the great hillside city of Segesta (▷ 101), and is still a busy fishing port. Castellammare was reputedly the inspiration of Mario Puzo's *The Godfather* and once had the worst reputation of any of Sicily's Mafia towns. It is more peaceful today, with elegant palaces and an Aragonese castle, from which the town takes its name.

✚ F3 🚹 Inside the castle, tel 0924 30217; Mon–Fri 9–1, 4–8 (3–7 in winter)
🍽 A good choice in town (€–€€)
🚉 Castellammare del Golfo station; bus shuttle to town

SAN VITO LO CAPO

www.sanvitoweb.com

The locals point out that to reach San Vito lo Capo by the only road that goes there, you have to pass through a town called Purgatory. So they think of their town as 'paradise'. For many Sicilians it's the top seaside spot, with a glorious beach of pinkish-white sand. Towards the end of September the town has a six-day *Couscous Fest* (▷ 105), with samplings, concerts and fireworks.

✉ E2 🚹 Via Savoia 61, tel 0924 974300; summer daily 9–1, 5–9; winter daily 9–1
🍽 A choice in town (€–€€) 🚌 From Trapani and Palermo

TRAPANI

If you can overlook Trapani's reputation as a major Sicilian Mafia centre, it's easy to fall in love with this handsome old town. Its medieval heart is like a sickle (the town's Greek name—Drepanon—means just that) jutting out into the sea. The Moorish alleys in the Casbah contrast with the baroque appearance of later streets, like Via Garibaldi, which is fringed by *palazzi* and churches.

✚ D3 🚹 Via San Francesco d'Assisi 27, tel 0923 545511; office closed to the public
🍽 Ai Lumi (€€; ▷ 106) 🚌 From Palermo and Agrigento 🚉 Trapani

A view over the harbour at Castellammare del Golfo

A cliff looms behind the beach at San Vito lo Capo

WESTERN SICILY

★

MORE TO SEE

Shopping

ANTONINO CATALANO

Among this shop's wide selection of souvenirs, there are bowls, jugs, platters and pottery in all shapes and sizes.

✚ E3 ✉ Via G. F. Guarnotto, Erice ☎ 0923 969 126 ⏰ Daily

LIBRERIA DEL CORSO

One of the best bookstores in this part of Sicily, this is the place to go if you want the lowdown on Sicily's past, its scenery and its art treasures. There's a good chance you'll find English-language versions.

✚ D3 ✉ Corso Vittorio Emanuele 61, Trapani ☎ 0923 26260 ⏰ Daily

PASTICCERIA GRAMMATICO

www.mariagrammatico.it
Maria Grammatico's world-famous pastry shop is in the mountain town of Erice. As well as fabled pastries, she sells *frutta martorana* (marzipan sweets), *cudduredde* (fig biscuits), *crostate di marmellata* (jam tarts), *mostaccioli di Erice* (Erice cinnamon biscuits) and other delicacies, along with wines and oils. Maria was the subject of the bestselling book *Bitter Almonds (Recollections and Recipes from a Sicilian Girlhood)* by Mary Taylor Simeti. It tells of Maria's childhood in a cloistered Erice orphanage, where

she learned to make hand-crafted pastries that were sold to customers from behind a grille in the convent wall.

✚ E3 ✉ Via Vittorio Emanuele 14, Erice ☎ 0923 869390

PERRONE CERAMICHE

The perfectly modelled ceramic replicas of traditional food sold here are very tempting as kitchen ornaments. The range of ceramics also includes some quirky designs.

✚ D3 ✉ Corso Vittorio Emanuele 106, Trapani ☎ 0923 29609

PLATIMIRO FIORENZA

Coral is traditionally used for jewellery-making in this area and you'll find some beautiful pieces in this fine shop. Platimiro

---

CERAMICS

Sicily has a strong ceramic tradition, with a reputation for colourful, decorative and practical pottery. Although Sciacca (▷ 87) and Caltagirone (▷ 64) are the island's 'Potteries' and have the widest choice and the most competitive prices, keep a lookout for originality and good prices in other areas of Sicily—especially in the far west. This area is also worth exploring for jewellery, the famous Marsala wine and Sicily's tastiest pastries.

---

also specializes in silver, creating exquisite replicas of exotic flowers.

✚ D3 ✉ Via Osorio 36, Trapani ☎ 0923 20785

STABILIMENTO FLORIO

If you are visiting Marsala, home of the famous wine, and want to buy some direct from the *baglio*, this is probably the best place to come. Enjoy a guided tour and a tasting before buying.

✚ D4 ✉ Lungomare Mediterranaeo, Marsala ☎ 0923 723846

STEFANIA MODE

www.stefaniamode.it
This is very much a local store, even though it has three outlets on the same street and the main one sells the latest trendy gear for women by the most famous Italian designers, including Armani, Cavalli, Fendi, Moschino and Prada. Clothes and accessories for young people are for sale at Via Torrearsa 95, and casual and sportswear at Via delle Arti 15.

✚ D3 ✉ Via delle Arti 15, 21 and 25 and Via Torrearsa 95, Trapani ☎ 0923 28938

TRAPANI MARKET

Browse through craftwork and clothes bargains at the busy market in Trapani, accessible from Pala Ilio, near the harbour.

✚ D3 ✉ By the port, Trapani ☎ 0923 29000 ⏰ Thu dawn to dusk

Entertainment and Activities

BAR CARAVELLE
Enjoy a beer or cocktail in this bar in the sedate hotel area of Marsala. The livelier seafront bars and restaurants aren't too far away.
🔲 D4 ☒ National Strasati 719, Marsala ☎ No phone number ⏰ Daily, until late

BAR TRITONE
The palm trees add to the ambience while you savour a drink in pleasant surroundings at this bar.
🔲 D3 ☒ Piazza Vittorio Emanuele 38, Trapani ☎ No phone number ⏰ Daily, until late

BIRRERIA ITALIA
This bar has an authentic Sicilian atmosphere. It serves bottled beers and snacks, and its streetside seating is ideal for watching the world go by. If you get really hungry, you can visit the nearby pizzeria.
🔲 D3 ☒ Via Torrearsa 5, Trapani ☎ 0923 21926 ⏰ Daily, until late (closed Sun off season)

CETARIA DIVING CENTRE
www.cetaria.com
If you want to do more than enjoy the beautiful views along the coast at Zingaro, you can dive with the Cetaria Diving Centre. There are courses for first-timers, but experienced divers can explore wrecks and underwater grottoes.
🔲 F3 ☒ Via Marco Polo 3, 91014 Scopello, Castellammare del Golfo ☎ 0924 541073 ⏰ Apr–Oct daily

CIRCOLO VELICO MARSALA
www.circolovelicomarsala.com
Circolo Velico is the yacht club at Marsala that hosts major summer events from the palm-fringed marina. It also organizes boat hire and small-boat tuition.
🔲 D4 ☒ Via Falco 5, Marsala ☎ 0923 713864 ⏰ Daily in summer

E & N CAFÉ
Located in the heart of Marsala's historic centre, this café-bar is very popular with the young and trendy and is one of the few places to stay open late in sleepy Marsala. As well as drinks, it serves an inviting array of ice creams and Sicilian sweets, including *cannoli* (oozing with ricotta and pistachio) and marzipan fruits.
🔲 D4 ☒ Via XI Maggio 130, Marsala ☎ 0923 951969 ⏰ Summer daily 7.30am–2am; winter Thu–Tue 7.30am–11pm

GORGONIA BLU DIVING
www.gorgoniablu.it
This friendly dive school offers a wide selection of courses, from beginner to expert, and all the equipment is available. It also runs excursions around the Egadi islands.
🔲 D4 ☒ Via Lipari 20, Marsala ☎ 347 353 1941 ⏰ Daily in summer

SEGESTA THEATRE
The third-century BC amphitheatre across from the Temple at Segesta (▷ 101) stages plays in odd-numbered years. Check with tourist offices in Palermo and Trapani for programmes.
🔲 F3 ☒ Via Segesta ☎ 0924 955841 ⏰ Biennially, mid-Jun to Sep

VILLA MARGHERITA,
www.lugliomusicaletrapanese.it
Every year in July the lovely gardens of Trapani's Villa Margherita become an open-air opera theatre for the *Luglio Musicale Trapanese*. Check with the local tourist office for the programme of events during your visit.
🔲 D3 ☒ Trapani ☎ Concert line 0923 21454 ⏰ Jul nightly at 9

CELEBRATING COUSCOUS

For six days in mid- to late September, San Vito lo Capo celebrates its famous dish, fish couscous. The International Couscous Festival includes free samples, dances to live music, concerts in Piazza Santuario and a dazzling midnight fireworks display on the last night. For more information, look up the website www.couscousfest.it.

Restaurants

AI LUMI (€€)

www.ailumi.it

The landlord himself, Riccardo Rizzo, buys all the ingredients fresh daily from the market and personally selects wines. This is an elegant restaurant with stylish furnishings and a rustic flavour.

➕ D3 ✉ Corso Vittorio Emanuele 75, Trapani ☎ 0923 872418 ⏰ Wed–Mon lunch and dinner. Closed 15 Jan–15 Feb

AL CAPO (€€)

www.pizzeriaalcapo.it

Very handy for the Museo Archeologico, this pizzeria-restaurant is in a restored warehouse.

➕ D4 ✉ Via Lungomare Boeo 38-40, Marsala ☎ 0923 956872 ⏰ Daily lunch and dinner (closed Tue off season)

LA BETTOLA DAL 1972 (€€)

www.ristorantelabettola.it

This excellent fish and seafood restaurant is very popular with the locals, with an extensive wine list that includes more than 200 Sicilian labels. It is run by the chef/patron Pietro Sardo, who personally discusses and prepares your feast.

➕ E5 ✉ Via F. Maccagnone 32, Mazara del Vallo ☎ 0923 946422 ⏰ Thu–Tue lunch and dinner

CANTINA SICILIANA (€€)

www.cantinasiciliana.it

A speciality here is the home-made *busiate* pasta served with *pesto al trapanese*—made with tomato, basil, garlic and almond—and fresh swordfish, accompanied by tiny tomatoes and capers from Pantelleria. It tastes as good as it sounds.

➕ D3 ✉ Via Giudecca 36, Trapani ☎ 0923 28673 ⏰ Daily lunch and dinner

MONTE SAN GIULIANO (€€€)

www.montesangiuliano.it

Local produce with a modern flavour is the speciality of this restaurant in the heart of lovely Erice, where you can eat in one of three rooms or outside in the courtyard.

➕ E3 ✉ Vicolo S. Rocco 7, Erice ☎ 0923 869595 ⏰ Tue–Sun lunch and dinner

PASTICCERIA GRAMMATICO (€)

www.mariagrammatico.it

A café-bar in the world-famous pastisserie (▷ 104), this place is unmissable.

➕ E3 ✉ Via Vittorio Emanuele 14, Erice ☎ 0923 869390 ⏰ Daily lunch

RISTORANTE EUBES (€€)

www.eubes.it

This delightful trattoria specializes in fish treats, home-made pasta and traditional Sicilian specialities. There is no menu, but the chef Gianfranco Conticello is a culinary wizard and rewards those with hearty appetites.

➕ D3 ✉ Contrada da Spagnola 228, Mozia ☎ 0923 996231 ⏰ Daily lunch and dinner

TRATTORIA GARIBALDI (€€)

Very near the cathedral in Marsala'a historic centre, this trattoria has a wide selection of antipasti. But look also for the catch-of-the-day grilled fish.

➕ D4 ✉ Piazza dell' Addolorata 35, Marsala ☎ 0923 953006 ⏰ Mon–Fri lunch and dinner, Sat dinner, Sun lunch

MARSALA WINE

Marsala has always been famous for its grapes, but it was English merchant John Woodhouse who first fortified Marsala wine and shipped it to Liverpool in 1773. It was an immediate success, endorsed in 1798 by Admiral Nelson himself. Today the wine houses retain their English names, but are mainly Italian-owned. Marsala can be sweet, spicy or dry–far more versatile than a dessert wine–and is used in many dishes, such as *pollo alla Marsala* (chicken in Marsala).

Where to Stay

Sicily has an excellent range of accommodation, with prices generally lower than on the mainland. Even top hotels in Palermo are cheaper than similar venues in other Italian cities.

Introduction

If you're looking for a place to stay, options range from sybaritic luxury in the grand hotels in Palermo and resorts like Taormina to the basic accommodation found in family-run, simple *pensione* and private rooms on farms.

Availability
There is an abundance of rooms in the main towns and tourist areas, but you should book ahead in summer, especially if you are heading inland, where accommodation is scarcer. One of the advantages of not booking ahead is that you can ask to check over the room before deciding to take it.

Prices
All types of accommodation are graded and the tariff is fixed by law—officially, that is. In reality, pricing is more variable, with mysterious extras often finding their way onto the bill during high season. Conversely, in low season, there is sometimes room for negotiating a lower price. If you're travelling with children, most hotels will put another bed in the room for an extra one-third of the room price.

Checking In and Checking Out
On arrival at the hotel you will be asked to hand over your passport, so the hotel can register you with the police (don't forget to ask for it back). Most hotels with three or more stars take credit cards, but you may find that simple *pensione* and bed-and-breakfasts may not.

UNDER CANVAS

● Sicily has around 90 official campsites, many of them large luxury affairs with swimming pools, shops, tennis courts and restaurants, though they are not open all year round. In fact, some open and close at will, according to business. For more information, look up www.camping.it.

● The campsites are usually heaving in high season with Italians on their summer holidays but quite uncrowded at other times. Touring Club Italiano (tel 02 852 6245; www.touringclub.it) publishes a campsite guide.

Flower-filled courtyards, ceramic-tile decoration and traditional furniture give a taste of Sicily

Budget Hotels

PRICES

Expect to pay up to €130 per night for a double room in a budget hotel.

ALBERGO SAVONA

www.hotelsavona.it
Enjoy a bit of grandeur at an excellent price. There are quiet rooms on three floors, and marble-capped stairs. Some rooms look out onto the Duomo, but ask for one with views of their quiet courtyard.
➕ Q5 ✉ Via Vittorio Emanuele 210, Catania ☎ 095 326982

IL BAROCCO

www.ilbarocco.it
Traditional rooms, tile floors and oak furnishing add elegance to this pretty, pink-washed hotel in the heart of Ragusa.
➕ P8 ✉ Via Santa Maria la Nuova 1, Ragusa Ibla (lower town) ☎ 0932 663105

CAMERE A SUD

www.camereasud.it
This chic little B&B is handy for Agrigento's Duomo and the Valley of the Temples. Book ahead for the best deals. Credit cards are not accepted.
➕ J6 ✉ Via Ficani 6, Agrigento ☎ 3496 384424

CARRUBELLA PARK

www.sicily-hotels.net/ CarrubellaParkHotel
Enjoy super views of Palermo and the sea in this great-value hilltop hotel. It is spacious, comfortable and clean, and has a solarium.
➕ G2 ✉ Via Umberto I 223, Monreale ☎ 0916 402187

DIANA BROWN

www.dianabrown.it
If you're planning to stay on Lipari, try this friendly family-run B&B. You'll find all the comforts you need, with plenty of advice on what to see.
➕ CII (inset map) ✉ Vico Himera 3, Lipari, Isole Eolie ☎ 0909 812584

HOTEL ALCESTE

www.hotelalceste.it
This small, family-run hotel has neat rooms and a restaurant serving tasty Sicilian cuisine. It's a 15-minute walk to Selinunte.
➕ F5 ✉ Via Alceste 21, Marinella di Selinunte ☎ 0924 46184

HOTEL GUTKOWSKI

www.guthotel.it
There's a lovely seaside setting for this Ortygia hotel, though not all

YOUTH HOSTELS

Sicily's youth hostels cost from €18 a night (the price rises in summer) and usually have good self-catering facilities. Official IYHF hostels are listed on the website www.ostellionline.org (you must be a member to log in). Independent hostels are listed on www.hostelworld.com/Sicily.

rooms have a sea view. It's boutique style, with cool decor.
➕ R7 ✉ Lungomare Vittorini 26, Siracusa ☎ 0931 465861

HOTEL JONIO

www.hoteljonio.eu
All the rooms have balconies at this family-run hotel, close to sandy beaches and 10 minutes' drive from Noto.
➕ Q8 ✉ Lungomare Lido, Marina di Noto, Noto ☎ 0931 812040

HOTEL LETIZIA

www.hotelletizia.com
At the top end of the budget price category, this elegant boutique hotel is a stone's throw from Palermo's Piazza Marina. But it's five floors up and there are no elevators.
➕ e4 ✉ Via Bottai 30, Palermo ☎ 091 589110

HOTEL MODERNO

www.hotelmodernoerice.it
This modern, well-equipped hotel in central Erice is in a charming 19th-century building with attractive furnishings. It's at the top end of the budget market.
➕ E3 ✉ Via Vittorio Emanuele 63, Erice ☎ 0923 869300

VILLA FAVORITA

www.villafavorita.com
Holiday in a villa here, or take a bungalow in the grounds.
➕ D4 ✉ Via Favorita 27, Marsala ☎ 0923 989100

Mid-Range Hotels

PRICES

Expect to pay between €130 and €230 per night for a double room in a mid-range hotel.

CENTRALE PALACE

www.centralepalacehotel.it
This luxurious hotel, in the Palazzo Tarallo, is decorated with frescoes and stucco work, and has antique furniture. The bedrooms are modern with sumptuous bathrooms, and there's also a roof garden, with one of the hotel's two splendid restaurants.
➕ d4 ✉ Corso Vittorio Emanuele 327, Palermo ☎ 091 336 666

COLLEVERDE PARK HOTEL

www.colleverdehotel.it
Halfway between Agrigento's Valle dei Templi archaeological zone and the city, with splendid views, this is a charming hotel with discreet decor, lovely artwork, lots of exposed beams and large picture windows. The staff are very helpful.
➕ J6 ✉ Via Panorámica dei Templi, Agrigento ☎ 092 229 555

DOMUS MARIAE

www.sistemia.it/domusmariae
This waterfront hotel is the only one in Siracusa that has its own chapel. It was once a Catholic school and is still owned by an order of Ursuline nuns. It's a pleasant hotel that offers simplicity and cleanliness, a peaceful reading room and rooftop terrace for sunbathing.
➕ R7 ✉ Via Vittorio Veneto 76, Ortygia, Siracusa ☎ 0931 24858/24854

GRAND ALBERGO SICILIA

www.hotelsiciliaenna.it
Don't be put off by this hotel's unprepossessing exterior. It is nicely furnished inside, with a marble reception area and a breakfast terrace.
➕ M5 ✉ Piazza Napoleone Colajanni 7, Enna ☎ 0935 500850

GRAND HOTEL ET DES PALMES

www.hotel-despalmes.it
This place has a grand history. It was originally home to the Ingham Whitaker family and had a secret passage to the Anglican church that stands in front. Wagner wrote *Parsifal* here and,

PRICE CONFUSION

Hotel prices in Sicily can be quite confusing. There are some elegant establishments in out-of-the-way spots that are in the budget price bracket yet are as good as more expensive central hotels. Even in Palermo, you can come across a reasonably priced place that should belong in the luxury bracket.

in the 1950s, Lucky Luciano—the *capo de capi* of the Cosa Nostra—notoriously attended a meeting of gangsters.
➕ e1 ✉ Via Roma 398, Palermo ☎ 091 602 8111

GRAND HOTEL PIAZZA BORSA

www.piazzaborsa.com
A stylish hotel in the heart of Palermo, the four-star Grand Hotel Piazza Borsa was launched in 2010 after the merger of three buildings. The central part of the structure was a 16th-century convent and the church of Mercedarian Fathers. The hotel lobby is bordered by the original cloisters.
➕ e4 ✉ Via dei Cartari 18, Palermo ☎ 091 320 075

HOTEL CARMINE

www.hotelcarmine.it
Modern furnishings with antique trimming decorate what is probably Marsala's most stylish hotel. It's very central, and many of the rooms have balconies overlooking the interior garden.
➕ D4 ✉ Piazza Cármine, Marsala ☎ 0923 711907

HOTEL MEDITERRANEO

www.hotelmediterraneoct.com
This modern, three-star Best Western hotel is in a residential area but quite close to the centre. It's basic, unfussy, comfortable and clean.
➕ Q5 ✉ Via Dottor Consoli 27, Catania ☎ 0953 25330

HOTEL VITTORIA
www.hotelvittoriatrapani.it
This well-placed hotel overlooks Trapani's Piazza Vittorio Emanuele. It's a comfortable, family-run hotel and, with the bus and rail stations nearby, a good base for exploring western Sicily.
✚ D3 ✉ Via Francesco Crispi 4, Trapani ☎ 0923 873044

LOCANDA DON SERAFINO
www.locandadonserafino.it
In the baroque heart of Ragusa, this was once a crumbling 18th-century town house. Now it has been beautifully restored as an intimate, chic and charming boutique hotel. The lovely Rosa family who run it also keep a superb wine cellar.
✚ P8 ✉ Via XI Febbraio 15, Ragusa ☎ 093 222 0065

RIVA DEL SOLE
www.rivadelsole.com
Considered the best hotel in Cefalù, the Riva del Sole is bright and well-equipped, with good accommodation and attentive service. It has an intimate bar, panoramic terrace and pleasant garden.
✚ K2 ✉ Via Lungomare G. Giardina 25, Cefalù ☎ 0921 421230 ⏰ Closed 31 Oct–23 Dec

SEA PALACE
www.cefaluseapalace.it
Many rooms have balconies looking out to sea at this smart hotel facing the beach at Cefalù.
✚ K2 ✉ Lungomare G. Giardina, Cefalù ☎ 0921 925011/6

TORRI PEPOLI
www.torripepoli.it
A castle watchtower on a rocky crag in Erice's upper town is now a charming, small and exclusive hotel. It has five rooms, individually furnished in neo-Gothic style but with excellent modern comforts. The views are among the best in Sicily.
✚ E3 ✉ Viale Conte Pepoli, Erice ☎ 0923 860117

VILLA BELVEDERE
www.villabelvedere.it
The rooms at the front of this friendly, family-run three-star hotel have sea views. There is a lovely

WHAT'S ON OFFER?
Hotels with three or more stars normally include air conditioning and heating in the price. Some may charge extra for breakfast, or not offer it at all. Just do what the Sicilians do and eat at a bar. Water is scarce in Sicily so few budget and mid-range hotels will have a bath, just a shower. Water pressure may vary from time to time and the water often drains through a hole in the centre of the bathroom—so don't leave clothes and towels where they can get wet.

cliffside terrace, as well as a swimming pool and garden.
✚ R3 ✉ Via Bagnoli Croce 79, Taormina ☎ 0942 23791 ⏰ Closed mid-Nov to Easter

VILLA CARLOTTA
www.villacarlotta.net
This smart, welcoming boutique hotel is set back from the San Domenico Palace (▷ 112) but enjoys the same spectacular sea views. The rooms are elegantly furnished, and breakfast is served on the rooftop terrace.
✚ R3 ✉ Via Pirandello 8, Taormina ☎ 0942 626058 ⏰ Closed 10 Jan–20 Feb

VILLA DUCALE
www.villaducale.com
In a villa in the quiet hamlet of Madonna della Rocca, this hotel has great views of Etna from its terrace. All rooms have a veranda, and there's a shuttle bus to Taormina and the beach.
✚ R3 ✉ Via Leonardo da Vinci 60, Madonna della Rocca, Taormina ☎ 0942 28153 ⏰ Closed Dec–Feb, but open over Christmas

VILLA MELIGUNIS
www.villameligunis.it
This former palace makes a comfortable base from which to explore the Aeolian Islands. The poolside rooftop restaurant offers views of Lipari.
✚ CII (inset map) ✉ Via Marti 7, Lipari, Isole Eolie ☎ 0909 812426 ⏰ Closed from end Oct–Easter

Luxury Hotels

BAGLIO DELLA LUNA

www.bagliodellaluna.com
There are beautiful views of the Valley of the Temples from this medieval building. It has the original courtyards, a 14th-century tower and elegantly furnished rooms that have a hint of bygone rural Sicily about them. There is also an outside breakfast terrace, a small pool and a highly popular restaurant.
✚ J6 ✉ Via Serafino Amabile Guastella 1, Agrigento
☎ 0922 511061

EREMO DELLA GIUBILIANA

www.eremodellagiubiliana.com
Located about 14km (9 miles) southwest of Ragusa towards the coast, this stylish hotel has rooms in the main building and five cottages in the grounds. It was once a fortified farmstead and former convent belonging to the Knights of Malta. It's hard to reach, though it does have its own private airstrip, from where excursions to offshore islands and Malta can be arranged.
✚ N8 ✉ Contrada Giubiliana, near Ragusa
☎ 0932 669119

EXCELSIOR GRAND HOTEL

www.excelsiorgrandhotel catania.com
The rooms of this prestigious hotel have opulent marble bathrooms and some have balconies that look to the lovely Piazza Giovanni Verga and out across to Mount Etna.
✚ Q5 ✉ Piazza G. Verga 39, Catania ☎ 0957 476111

GRAND HOTEL TIMEO

www.grandhoteltimeo.com
Taormina's grandest hotel has a location to match: in front of the Greek Theatre. Rooms have balconies or a terrace, and there's a pool, gym and terrace restaurant.
✚ R3 ✉ Via Teatro Greco 5, Taormina ☎ 0942 628501
🚫 Closed 15 Nov–Easter

HOTEL ROMA

www.hotelroma.sr.it
One of the finest hotels in Siracusa, Roma also has one of the area's best restaurants, Vittorini. It has

rooms adapted for people with disabilities.
✚ R7 ✉ Via Roma 66, Siracusa ☎ 0931 465626

KEMPINSKI HOTEL

www.kempinski-sicily.com
Among palms, olive groves and vineyards, with gardens, fountains, flowers and gazebos, this hotel on the outskirts of Mazara del Vallo was the first five-star hotel in this part of Sicily. It has pools, tennis courts, a spa and a beach club.
✚ E5 ✉ Via Salemi, Giardino di Costanza, Mazara del Vallo ☎ 0923 675000

ROCCO FORTE VERDURA GOLF & SPA RESORT

www.roccofortecollection.com
Near the fishing village of Sciacca, this stunning addition to the Rocco Forte portfolio opened in 2009. All the 203 rooms and suites have sea views and private terraces and there is a private beach and state-of-the-art spa.
✚ G5 ✉ Contrada Verdura, Sciacca ☎ 0925 998180

SAN DOMENICO PALACE

www.sandomenico.thi.it
This former Dominican monastery is one of Italy's greatest hotels. It offers impeccable service, beautiful rooms and a spectacular view of the sea and Mount Etna.
✚ R3 ✉ Piazza San Domenico 5, Taormina
☎ 0942 613111

This section gives you the practical information you need to plan your visit to Sicily and to make the most of your time on the island.

Need to Know

Planning Ahead

When to Go

The peak time is sizzlingly hot July and August, when many holidaymakers arrive from mainland Italy. But from April to June and September to October the weather is usually good. Spring brings carpets of wild flowers, while autumn is full of harvest festivals.

TIME

L Sicily is one hour ahead of the UK, six hours ahead of New York and nine hours ahead of Los Angeles.

AVERAGE DAILY MAXIMUM TEMPERATURES											
JAN	FEB	MAR	APR	MAY	JUN	JUL	AUG	SEP	OCT	NOV	DEC
12°C	13°C	13°C	16°C	19°C	22°C	26°C	26°C	24°C	21°C	17°C	13°C
54°F	55°F	56°F	60°F	66°F	72°F	78°F	79°F	75°F	69°F	62°F	56°F

Spring (March to May) can be wet and breezy in March, but in April and May the island is ablaze with flowers and the first swimmers put their toes in the water.

Summer (June to August) brings strong, bleaching rays of sun and the sea is now warm and a magnet in high summer for most Sicilians and visitors.

Autumn (September to October) temperatures remain high for the early part and the sea remains warm, but by October there is a risk of coastal storms.

Winter (November to February) high winds, including the *scirocco* North African wind, blow and rainfall is at its highest. In midwinter, the mountains can be blanketed in snow.

WHAT'S ON

January *Festa Nazionale della Befana* (6 Jan).

February *Sagra del Mandorlo in Fiore,* Agrigento (early Feb): almond blossom festival.

Feast of Saint Agata, Catania (3–5 Feb): spectacular processions and feasting.

Carnevale (week before Ash Wednesday): towns erupt into parades and feasting.

March/April *Pasqua* (Easter): processions and passion plays (▷ 77).

May *Infiorata,* Caltagirone (last two weeks of May): flower festival (▷ 64).

Festival of Greek Classical Drama, Siracusa (May–Jun).

June *Arts festival* in Teatro Greco, Taormina (Jun–Aug).

Taormina Film Fest, Taormina (one week in Jun, ▷ 59).

July *Feast of Santa Rosalia,* Palermo (10–15 Jul).

Music Festival, Erice (2nd week in Jul).

Estate Musicale Trapanese (all month): outdoor opera at Villa Margherita, Trapani.

U Fistinu, Palermo (12–15 Jul): parades and fireworks.

Estate Ennese, Enna (Jul–Aug): opera festival.

August *Agosto Ibleo* (all month): celebrations in Ragusa Ibla.

Ferragosto (Assumption Day, 13–15 Aug): processions, music and fireworks, at their most colourful in Palermo.

September *International Couscous Festival,* San Vito lo Capo (▷ 105).

November *Ognissanti/Festa dei Morti* (All Souls Day/Day of the Dead, 1 Nov): people pay homage to their dearly departed.

December *Santa Lucia,* Siracusa (13 Dec): processions and fireworks.

Christmas in Sicily lasts from 24 December to 6 January. Churches light up with spectacular images of the Nativity.

Useful Websites

www.addiopizzo.org
Inaugurated in 2004, the Addio Pizzo (goodbye protection money) organization supports businesses that encourage Mafia-free commerce, refusing to pay the bribes. It's estimated that more than 80 per cent of Sicilian businesses pay protection money to the Cosa Nostra, so this website guides you towards those that refuse to pay for a *pizzo* of the action.

www.agriturismosicilia.it
Here you'll find a list of the agritourism properties on the island and information on where you can join in with activities such as the harvest or watching the pressing of olive oil.

www.apt.catania.it
This website provides information on Catania and its province, with useful advice on getting around and accommodation options.

www.bestofsicily.com
This very informative site covers culture, tourist sights, history, food and wine. It also has the Best of Sicily Online Magazine, packed full of interesting features.

www.loveitaly.co.uk
The website of the Association of British Tour Operators to Italy.

www.palermotourism.com
This website covers all aspects of Palermo and its province, with information on attractions, accommodation, food and transport.

www.parcs.it
Information on all the natural parks in Italy.

www.regione.sicilia.it/turismo
The website of the Sicilian Regional Tourist Board has information on local food, culture, events and more.

INTERNET ACCESS
There are plenty of places where you can access the internet on the island, mostly in the bigger towns and cities. Many municipal offices have internet rooms alongside their libraries and there are also cyber cafés. You will normally be asked to show your ID at public internet points. Prices vary but expect to pay about €5 an hour, although free WiFi access is increasingly available in bars and in some hotels.

INTERNET CAFÉS
Aboriginal Internet Café
www.aboriginalcafe.com
d2
Via Spinuzza 51, Palermo
091 662 2229
Daily 10am–3am
€3.50 per hour, including free coffee

Las Vegas Internet Café
R3
Salita Alexander Humboldt 7, Taormina
0942 24059
Daily 10am–1am
€2 for 20 mins, then €0.10 per minute

Getting There

NEED TO KNOW GETTING THERE

ENTRY REQUIREMENTS

UK and other EU citizens do not need a visa, but do need a valid passport for entry to Italy. Citizens of Australia, Canada, New Zealand and the US do not require a visa for stays of up to 90 days. If you are planning to stay longer than 90 days, you must register in person at the local Foreigners' Office and be issued with a certificate. Legally you are required to register with the police within three days of entering Sicily. However, if you are staying at a hotel this will be done for you. Always check the latest requirements before you travel.

INSURANCE

EU nationals are entitled to reduced-cost emergency medical treatment on presentation of a European Health Insurance Card (EHIC). Obtain one before travelling (www.ehic.org.uk for UK citizens). US travellers should check their health coverage before departure. In all cases, comprehensive travel and medical insurance is advised. Always ensure you have full insurance when hiring a car. If any of your possessions are stolen, you need to complete a report at the police *(polizia)* station.

AIRPORTS

Sicily has three international airports: Palermo Falcone e Borsellino is 31km (19 miles) west of Palermo; Catania Fontanarossa is 7km (4 miles) southeast of Catania; and Trapani Birgi is 15km (9 miles) southeast of Trapani.

ARRIVING BY AIR
Some visitors fly first to the Italian mainland hubs of Rome or Milan and then take a connecting flight to Sicily, usually to Catania or Palermo.

ARRIVING AT PALERMO
From Palermo's Falcone e Borsellino airport (tel 800 541 880; www.gesap.it) an airport bus (tel 0645 2400) departs every 30 minutes (5am–11pm). You can buy tickets on board for €5 and the journey time is about 55 minutes. The bus stops in Palermo at Viale Lazio, Via Libertà, Piazza Politeama and the main train station. There's also a train service, the Trinacria Express (tel 0540 2340) that takes around 40 minutes. Trains leave around every 90 minutes (5.30am–10.10pm) from the airport terminal's lower level and tickets cost €6. By taxi, the journey takes about 25 minutes and costs around €50. The rate increases after 8pm.

ARRIVING AT CATANIA
From Catania Fontanarossa (tel 095 723 9111; www.aeroporto.catania.it) the AMT Alibus

goes into Catania, with several stops, including the main train station. The journey takes 15 minutes and costs €1, running from 5am to midnight. There are also buses from the airport to Taormina, costing €5 (7am–7.30pm; journey time 50 minutes). A taxi from the airport to Catania centre costs around €25 and takes 15 minutes.

ARRIVING AT TRAPANI
Trapani Birgi airport (tel 0923 842502; www. airgest.it) is served by budget airlines and is western Sicily's main hub. There are regular bus connections to Trapani centre, costing €3.50 (8.15am–11.15pm; journey time 25 mins). There are also less regular bus links to Marsala (15km/9 miles south) for €3.50 and to Agrigento for €10.60. Travel time to Palermo is just over an hour. From Trapani airport there are flights to the islands of Pantelleria and Lampedusa.

ARRIVING BY FERRY
The main Sicilian ports are Palermo in the northwest, Trapani in the west and Messina in the northeast. The major connection from the Italian mainland at Reggio di Calabria is to Messina (12km/7.5 miles across the straits; journey time 15 mins on the hydrofoil and 25 mins on the regular ferry). Ustica (tel 0923 873813; www.usticalines.it) operates hydrofoils and ferries from Reggio di Calabria to Messina. Other routes to Sicily are from Naples, Pisa (tuna), Livorno, Civitavecchia (Rome), Cagliari (Sardinia) and from Malta and Tunisia. SNAV (tel 081 428 5555; www.snav.it) and Tirrenia (tel 02 2630 2803; www.tirrenia.it) have regular crossings from Naples to Palermo (around 10.5 hours) and SNAV has crossings between Civitavecchia and Palermo and between Naples and the Aeolian Isles. You can check schedules, fares and book tickets on www.directferries.co.uk or www.viamare.com. If you are planning to travel in high season, book longer crossings weeks in advance.

ITALIAN TOURIST OFFICES AT HOME

UK
www.enit.it
☎ 020 7408 1254

US
www.italiantourism.com
☎ 212/245-5095

Canada
www.italiantourism.com
☎ 416/925-4882

Australia
www.italiantourism.com.au
☎ 02/9262 1666

CAR HIRE
Car hire firms with desks at the airports include:
Avis ☎ 800 331 1212 or 02 7541 9761; www.avis.com
Hertz ☎ 800 654 3131 or 199 112211; www.hertz.com
Maggiore ☎ 095 536927 or 06 229 1530; www.maggiore.it

Getting Around

VISITORS WITH DISABILITIES

Sicily is not well geared to travellers with disabilities. That said, Sicilians will generally go out of their way to be helpful, but the mountainous terrain of the island, steep inclines within many towns, reckless driving and narrow, cobbled streets can be daunting. However, many new and restored hotels and restaurants have a legal requirement to offer wheelchair ramps and wider doors and most of the larger and more upmarket hotels do now have good facilities. Contact specialists such as Society for Accessible Travel and Hospitality (www.sath. org) and Accessible Italy (www.accessibleitaly.com) when planning your trip.

TAXIS

Taxis are expensive and additional tariffs are added 10pm–7am and on national holidays. Taxis rarely stop if you hail them on the street, but you will find taxi ranks in the big towns and cities. Enquire on the likely fare before you commit yourself. If you call a taxi by phone the meter starts running from the time the taxi leaves. In Palermo, you can call Autoradiotaxi (tel 091 513 311/512 727). In Catania, try CST (tel 095 330 966).

AIR
There are domestic flights from Palermo and Trápani to the Pelagie Islands and Pantelleria with Meridiana (www.meridiana.it) and Air One (www.flayairone.it) in summer.

ISLAND BUSES
Buses are the most popular means of public transport on Sicily. However, timings can be erratic and the buses often go at limited times tied to market or school times. SAIS Autolinee (tel 091 616028 in Palermo or 095 536168 in Catania; www.saisautolinee.it) offers services from Palermo to Messina, Catania and Siracusa. Cuffaro (tel 091 616 1510; www.cuffaro.info) links Palermo in the north with Agrigento in the south. Interbus (tel 094 2625301; www. interbus.it) has services between Catania, Messina, Taormina and Siracusa. SAIS Trasporti (tel 095 5366168; www.saistrasporti.it) and Giuntabus (tel 090 673782; www.giuntabus. com) also offer routes.

CITY BUSES
Buses within cities are usually frequent and reliable. You need to purchase a ticket before boarding, from newsagents, *tabaccherie* (tobacconists) and some bars (around €1.20). You must validate your ticket in the machine when you board the bus and the ticket is then valid for 60–90 minutes from the time it is stamped. Boarding a bus without a ticket or failure to stamp it could earn you a €50 fine. (Some ticket inspectors are not noted for their diplomacy or tact and they get a bonus for each fine collected.) Sometimes a city will offer a 24-hour transit ticket that can save you money if you plan to use the bus network extensively.

DRIVING
For freedom and convenience, renting a car is the best way to explore. However, you will need nerves of steel as the Sicilians truly deserve their reputation for recklessness on the road. All the major international car hire companies have

outlets at the airports (▷ 117), although it is
essential to book as early as possible for popular
destinations at busy times of the year—and it is
usually cheaper to arrange a fly-drive deal before
you leave home. For most companies you need
to be at least 21 years old and there may be
a young-driver surcharge for those under 25.
Insurance is compulsory and you would be wise
to take out fully comprehensive insurance to
cover you for any scrapes that occur.

RULES OF THE ROAD
● Drive on the right.
● Dipped headlights should be used at all times
outside built-up areas.
● The speed limit is 50kph (31mph) in urban
areas, 110kph (68mph) on main roads and
130kph (80mph) on motorways *(autostrade)*,
for which there is a toll.
● Seat belts are compulsory for all passengers.
Children must have a suitable restraint system.
Children under 1.5m (4.9ft) must sit in the back
of the car.
● There are severe penalties for drink driving.
Never drink and drive.
● On-the-spot fines for minor traffic offences are
expensive—usually around €200. Get a receipt if
you incur one.

TRAINS
All the major cities have rail links, but Sicily's
rail network is patchy and services can be slow.
The train service is usually better on the east of
the island than the west, and the coast is better
served than the interior. Bear in mind in Sicily
that stations can be quite a distance from the
town they serve. However, fares are low and
trains usually run on time. You must validate
your ticket at the yellow stamping machine on
the platforms before boarding. Failure to do this
can cost you an instant fine. Trains are operated
by Italian State Railways (Ferrovie dello Stato).
Check the FS website for timetables and to
book online (www.trenitalia.com). The website
has a useful English-language version.

MAPS
Tourist offices and hotel
reception desks give free
island maps and street plans.
The Touring Club Italiano
produces a detailed road
map of Sicily (1:200,000),
(www.touringclub.com),
which is available from
bookshops.

TOURS
Hop-on-hop-off city sightseeing tours in open-top
buses with a multilingual
commentary are a good
way of orienting yourself. In
Palermo, City Sightseeing (tel
091 589 429; www.palermo.
city sightseeing.it) has
regular departures on two
lines (A and B) from Piazza
Politeama every 30–60
minutes. Buy tickets on
board (adult €20, child €10).
For details of excursions from
Catania look up www.
cataniacittametropolitana.it).
You will find many options
for visiting Mount Etna,
including day trips by
Geo Etna Explorer (www.
geoetnaexplorer.it)

NEED TO KNOW GETTING AROUND

Essential Facts

- Police 112
- Fire brigade 115
- Ambulance 118

MONEY

The euro (€) is the official currency. Notes come in denominations of 5, 10, 20, 50, 100, 200 and 500. Coins are issued in denominations of 1, 2, 5, 10, 20 and 50 cents and 1 and 2 euros. Credit cards are accepted in larger hotels, restaurants and shops, but cash is preferred in smaller establishments and remote places. ATM (cashpoint) machines are widespread in the large towns and cities. Banks will change foreign currency and traveller's cheques.

€5

€10

€50

€100

CUSTOMS

EU nationals do not have to declare goods imported for their personal use, although it is wise to remain within the country's guidelines for what is considered personal use. The limits for non-EU visitors are 200 cigarettes or 50 cigars or 250g of tobacco; 2 litres of still table wine; 1 litre of spirits or strong liqueurs (over 22 per cent alcohol) or 2 litres of fortified or sparkling wine; 60ml of perfume.

ELECTRICITY

- The current is 220 volts AC (50 cycles). Most plugs have two round pins. UK visitors will need an adaptor. US visitors need an adaptor and a transformer for 100–120 volt devices.

ETIQUETTE

- *La bella figura* (a good image) is expected and smart-casual dress is the norm. Dress up at night for fashionable restaurants and clubs.
- Cover up arms and legs when visiting churches.
- Open displays of drunkenness are greatly frowned upon.

MEDICAL TREATMENT

- Hotels have details of the nearest English-speaking doctor or dentist.
- Pharmacies *(farmacie),* identified by a large green cross, open Mon–Sat 9–1, 4–8. Details of late-night and Sunday duty chemists are posted in pharmacy windows.
- Pharmacists are highly trained and can sell some drugs that require prescriptions in other countries—but always take supplies of your own prescription drugs.

NATIONAL HOLIDAYS

- 1 Jan: New Year's Day
- 6 Jan: Epiphany
- Mar/Apr: Easter Monday
- 25 Apr: Liberation Day
- 1 May: Labour Day
- 2 Jun: Republic Day

- 15 Aug: *Ferragosto* (Feast of the Assumption)
- 1 Nov: All Saints' Day
- 8 Dec: Feast of the Immaculate Conception
- 25 Dec: Christmas Day
- 26 Dec: St. Stephen's Day

OPENING HOURS
- Shops typically open Tue–Sat 8 or 9 to 1 and then from 4 to 7 or 8. Food shops are also open on Mon, as are shops in holiday resorts. Shops in larger towns and cities may be open all day *(orario continuato)*. Banks generally open Mon–Fri 8.30–1.30, 3–4.
- Post Offices open Mon–Sat 8.30–6.30 at main branches, shorter hours in provincial areas.
- Museums and churches generally open 9–1, 4–6, but hours are variable and many close on Monday or at the whim of custodians.
- Archaeological sites usually open at 9 until one hour before sunset.

SENSIBLE PRECAUTIONS
Violence against tourists is unusual in Sicily, but petty crime such as pickpocketing, bag-snatching and theft from cars is common.
- Don't flaunt expensive jewellery or equipment.
- If your hotel has a safe, use it.
- Never leave anything visible in the car.
- Be especially wary of pickpockets in markets and busy streets.
- Stick to well-lit streets at night.

TELEPHONES
- Mobile coverage is good but it's usually cheaper to use a public phone with a phone-card *(carta telefonica)* available from newsstands and *tabaccherie*.
- To call abroad, dial 00 followed by:
UK 44
US/Canada 1
Irish Republic 353
Australia 61
- The international code for Italy is 39.

EMBASSIES AND CONSULATES

UK Consulate
✉ Via Cavour 117, Palermo
☎ 091 326 412
UK Embassy
✉ Via XX Settembre 80A, Rome ☎ 06 4220 0001
Irish Embassy
✉ Piazza di Campitelli 3, Rome ☎ 06 697 9121
US Consulate
✉ Via Vaccarini 1, Palermo
☎ 091 305 857

TOILETS
Sometimes there's a charge to use public toilets *(bagni* or *gabinetti)*, or an attendant who expects a tip. Off the tourist trail, public toilets are rare and you'll have to rely on toilets in bars and hotels (but buy a drink there first).

TRAVELLING WITH CHILDREN
Children are doted upon and your welcome everywhere will be all the warmer for having them in your company. But do make sure they are well-protected from the sun with sun block and sun hats. Pharmacies stock all baby care products. Children will love Sicilian ice cream but, be warned, they'll also be tempted by an awful lot of the sticky treats favoured by sweet-toothed Sicilians.

Language

The Sicilian language bears only a passing resemblance to Italian (▷ panel, 4). However, you will be understood if you speak Italian and you may find the following Italian words and phrases helpful during your visit. Once you have mastered a few basic rules, Italian is an easy language to speak: It is phonetic and, unlike English, particular combinations of letters are always pronounced the same way. The stress is usually on the penultimate syllable, but if the word has an accent, this is where the stress falls.

USEFUL WORDS AND PHRASES		NUMBERS	
yes	sì	0	zero
no	no	1	uno
please	per piacere/per favore	2	due
thank you	grazie	3	tre
you're welcome	prego	4	quattro
excuse me!	scusi!	5	cinque
where	dove	6	sei
here	qui	7	sette
there	là	8	otto
when	quando	9	nove
now	adesso	10	dieci
later	più tardi	11	undici
why	perchè	12	dodici
who	chi	13	tredici
may I/can I	posso	14	quattordici
What is the time?	Che ore sono?	15	quindici
When do you open/close?	A che ora apre/chiude?	16	sedici
Do you speak English?	Parla inglese?	17	diciassette
I don't understand	Non capisco	18	diciotto
Please repeat that	Può ripetere?	19	diciannove
My name is…	Mi chiamo…	20	venti
Hello, pleased to meet you	Piacere	21	ventuno
Good morning	Buongiorno	22	ventidue
Good afternoon/evening	Buonasera	30	trenta
Goodbye	Arrivederci	40	quaranta
How are you?	Come sta?	50	cinquanta
I'm sorry	Mi dispiace	60	sessanta
See you later	A più tardi	70	settanta
		80	ottanta
		90	novanta
		100	cento
		1000	mille
		million	milione

NEED TO KNOW LANGUAGE

122

POST AND TELEPHONE

One stamp, please	*Un francobollo, per favore*
I'd like to send this by airmail	*Vorrei spedire questo per posta aerea*
Can you direct me to a public phone?	*Dov'è il telefono pubblico più vicino?*
Where can I buy a phone card?	*Dove posso comprare una carta telefonica?*
I'd like to speak to…	*Vorrei parlare con…*

GETTING AROUND

Where is the train station?	*Dov'è la stazione ferroviaria?*
Does this train/ bus go to…?	*È questo il treno/ l'autobus?*
Where can I buy a ticket?	*Dove si comprano i biglietti?*
Please can I have a single/ return ticket to…	*Un biglietto di andata/andata e ritorno per…*
When is the first/ last bus to…?	*Quando c'è il primo/l'ultimo autobus per…?*
I would like a standard/first class ticket to…	*Un biglietto di seconda/prima classe per…*
How much is the journey?	*Quanto costerà il viaggio?*
Turn on the meter	*Accenda il tassametro*
I'd like to get out here, please	*Vorrei scendere qui, per favore*
Could you wait for me please?	*Mi può aspettare, per favore?*
Is this the way to…?	*È questa la strada per…?*
Where is the timetable?	*Dov'è l'orario?*

RESTAURANTS

I'd like to reserve a table for…people at…	*Vorrei prenotare un tavolo per…persone a…*
A table for…, please.	*Un tavolo per…, per favore.*
Could we sit there?	*Possiamo sederci qui?*
Where are the toilets?	*Dove sono i gabinetti?*
Could we see the menu/wine list?	*Possiamo vedere il menù/la lista dei vini?*
What is the house special?	*Qual è la specialità della casa?*
I am a vegetarian	*Sono vegetariano/a*
I'd like…	*Vorrei…*
I ordered…	*Ho ordinato…*
Can I have the bill, please?	*Il conto, per favore?*

Timeline

WORLD CROSSROADS

For millennia Sicily has been the world's crossroads and a threshold to Europe for every conceivable invader. After peaceful colonists, the Greeks came in the eighth century BC and then the Romans, Goths and Vandals, Byzantines, Normans, Austrians, Spanish and Bourbons. It was in Sicily that Garibaldi landed at the start of the Unification and the Allies began the liberation of Europe during World War II.

A BRIDGE TOO FAR

Plans for a bridge across the Straits of Messina, linking Sicily with mainland Italy, have been around since Roman times—with little hope of materialization. Until now, maybe. A 2002 plan to go ahead was ditched in 2006 after protests from environmentalists and seismologists. But in 2009 plans for the world's largest suspension bridge were announced, so it may yet happen.

6000–1200BC Sikan, Elymian and Sikel agricultural societies emerge.

735BC Greek settlers arrive on the east coast. They establish Siracusa, Selinunte and Agrigento.

650–580BC Phoenician colonies build up on the west coast.

5th–3rd century BC The Greek Golden Age: Greek Sicily basks in the glory, influence and culture of Ancient Greece.

397BC The Greeks expel the Phoenicians.

AD264–410 The Romans occupy Sicily and exploit the island for grain and slaves.

5th century Goths and Vandals occupy.

535 Start of 300 years of Byzantine rule.

827 The Muslim invasion heralds the next Golden Age, including the introduction of new farming methods.

1040 The Normans invade.

1091 Roger de Hauteville takes all Sicily and is proclaimed King Roger I. Norman rule lasts until 1189 and is the island's third Golden Age.

1198–1250 Sicily becomes part of the Holy Roman Empire.

1291–1720 The island suffers systematic impoverishment under Spanish rule.

1669 Etna erupts, devastating Catania.

1693 An earthquake kills 50,000 people.

1720 The bourbons become rulers.

1860 Garibaldi lands in Marsala and takes Palermo. Sicily becomes part of the new Italy.

1866–1890 Emergence of the *Fasci Siciliani* movement to protect the poor and exploited—which is to evolve into the Mafia.

1908 Messina earthquake kills 80,000.

1930–1939 Mussolini cracks down on the Mafia.

1943 Allied forces enter Sicily in a bid to regain control of Italy and the rest of Europe.

1947 Launch of Sicily's Regional Parliament.

1970 An anti-Mafia drive heralds the start of murders and *maxiprocessi* (trials) in the 1980s.

1992 Two prosecutors are killed by a Mafia car bomb.

2010 More than 40 suspects are arrested in police swoops as part of Sicily's anti-Mafia campaign.

EMIGRATION

In terms of world influence, the Sicilian diaspora has been significant. Between 1890 and 1920, 25 per cent of the population left Sicily and became economic migrants. Further large-scale emigration took place between 1950 and 1970. There are districts known as Little Sicily and Little Palermo in US cities, and Sicilian culture, including the music and cuisine, is in evidence all over the world. In America, the Sicilian influence in the world of jazz is very much recognized. But then so too is their contribution to the darker side of life in the shape of the Mafia, as portrayed in films like *The Godfather*.

Sicily has plenty of Greek and Roman remains to remind visitors of its ancient history; cathedrals, such as the Duomo in Cefalù (below), represent a more recent past

Index

TWINPACK
Sicily

WRITTEN BY Adele Evans
COVER DESIGN Catherine Murray
DESIGN WORK Lesley Mitchell
INDEXER Marie Lorimer
IMAGE RETOUCHING AND REPRO Jackie Street
PROJECT EDITOR Kathryn Glendenning
SERIES EDITOR Marie-Claire Jefferies

Colour separation by AA Digital Department
Printed and bound by Leo Paper Products, China

A CIP catalogue record for this book is available from the British Library.

ISBN 978-0-7495-6809-2

We have tried to ensure accuracy in this guide, but things do change, so please let us know if you have any comments at travelguides@theAA.com.

Published by AA Publishing, a trading name of AA Media Limited, whose registered office is Fanum House, Basing View, Basingstoke, Hampshire RG21 4EA. Registered number 06112600.

Front cover image: AA/N Setchfield
Back cover images: (i) AA/N Setchfield; (ii) AA/C Sawyer; (iii) AA/N Setchfield; (iv) AA/N Setchfield

A04027
Maps in this title produced from map data © New Holland Publishing (South Africa) (Pty) Ltd 2008

The Automobile Association would like to thank the following photographers, companies and picture libraries for their assistance in the preparation of this book.

Abbreviations for the picture credits are as follows – (t) top; (b) bottom; (c) centre; (l) left; (r) right; (AA) AA World Travel Library.

1 AA/C Sawyer; **2** AA/N Setchfield; **3** AA/N Setchfield; **4t** AA/N Setchfield; **4c** AA/N Setchfield; **5t** AA/N Setchfield; **5c** AA/C Sawyer; **6t** AA/N Setchfield; **6cl** AA/C Sawyer; **6c** AA/N Setchfield; **6cr** AA/N Setchfield; **6bl** AA/N Setchfield; **6bc** AA/C Sawyer; **6br** AA/N Setchfield; **7t** AA/N Setchfield; **7cl** AA/N Setchfield; **7c** AA/N Setchfield; **7cr** AA/N Setchfield; **7bl** AA/C Sawyer; **7bc** AA/N Setchfield; **7br** AA/N Setchfield; **8** AA/N Setchfield; **9** AA/N Setchfield; **10t** AA/N Setchfield; **10/11ct** AA/N Setchfield; **10cr** AA/C Sawyer; **10br** AA/N Setchfield; **11t** AA/N Setchfield; **11cl** AA/N Setchfield; **11bl** AA/N Setchfield; **12t** AA/N Setchfield; **12tr** AA/N Setchfield; **12tcr** AA/N Setchfield; **12cr** AA/N Setchfield; **12br** AA/N Setchfield; **13t** AA/N Setchfield; **13tl** © CuboImages srl/Alamy; **13tcl** AA/C Sawyer; **13cl** © Gianni Muratore/Alamy; **13bl** AA/J A Tims; **14t** AA/N Setchfield; **14tr** AA/N Setchfield; **14tcr** AA/N Setchfield; **14cr** AA/C Sawyer; **14br** AA/C Sawyer; **15t** AA/N Setchfield; **15b** AA/N Setchfield; **16t** AA/N Setchfield; **16tr** AA/C Sawyer; **16tcr** AA/N Setchfield; **16cr** AA/C Saywer; **16br** AA/N Setchfield; **17t** AA/N Setchfield; **17tl** AA/N Setchfield; **17cl** AA/N Setchfield; **17bl** AA/N Setchfield; **18t** AA/N Setchfield; **18tr** AA/N Setchfield; **18cr** AA/C Saywer; **18br** AA/N Setchfield; **19i** AA/N Setchfield; **19ii** AA/N Setchfield; **19iii** AA/C Saywer; **19iv** © Barry Mason/Alamy; **19v** AA/N Setchfield; **19vi** AA/N Setchfield; **20/21** AA/N Setchfield; **24l** AA/C Sawyer; **24c** AA/C Sawyer; **24r** AA/N Setchfield; **25l** AA/C Sawyer; **25r** AA/C Sawyer; **26l** AA/N Setchfield; **26r** AA/N Setchfield; **26/27** AA/N Setchfield; **27t** AA/N Setchfield; **27c** AA/N Setchfield; **28t** AA/N Setchfield; **28bl** AA/N Setchfield; **28br** AA/N Setchfield; **29t** AA/N Setchfield; **29bl** AA/C Saywer; **29br** AA/N Setchfield; **30** AA/C Sawyer; **31** AA/N Setchfield; **32** AA/N Setchfield; **33** AA/N Setchfield; **34** AA/C Sawyer; **35** AA/C Sawyer; **38l** AA/C Sawyer; **38r** AA/N Setchfield; **39l** AA/N Setchfield; **39r** AA/N Setchfield; **40l** AA/N Setchfield; **40c** AA/N Setchfield; **40r** AA/N Setchfield; **41t** AA/N Setchfield; **41b** AA/N Setchfield; **42** AA/N Setchfield; **43** AA/N Setchfield; **44** AA/C Sawyer; **45** AA/N Setchfield; **48l** © Westend61 GmbH/Alamy; **48r** © CuboImages srl/Alamy; **49l** AA/C Sawyer; **49r** AA/C Sawyer; **50l** AA/N Setchfield; **50c** AA/N Setchfield; **50r** AA/N Setchfield; **51l** AA/C Sawyer; **51r** AA/N Setchfield; **52t** AA/N Setchfield; **52b** © Witold Skrypczak/Alamy; **53t** AA/N Setchfield; **53l** AA/N Setchfield; **53r** AA/N Setchfield; **54t** AA/N Setchfield; **54b** © PCL/Alamy; **55** © CuboImages srl/Alamy; **56** © CuboImages srl/Alamy; **57** AA/C Sawyer; **58** AA/N Setchfield; **59** AA/N Setchfield; **60** AA/C Sawyer; **61** AA/N Setchfield; **64l** AA/N Setchfield; **64r** AA/N Setchfield; **65** AA/N Setchfield; **66** AA/C Sawyer; **66/67** AA/N Setchfield; **67t** AA/N Setchfield; **67c** AA/C Sawyer; **68** © Brenda Kean/Alamy; **69l** AA/N Setchfield; **69c** AA/N Setchfield; **69r** AA/C Saywer; **70** AA/C Sawyer; **70/71** AA/N Setchfield; **71** AA/N Setchfield; **72** © Peter Scholey/Alamy; **73t** AA/N Setchfield; **73bl** AA/J A Tims; **73br** AA/N Setchfield; **74t** AA/N Setchfield; **74bl** AA/N Setchfield; **74br** AA/N Setchfield; **75** AA/N Setchfield; **76** AA/N Setchfield; **77** AA/N Setchfield; **78** AA/C Sawywer; **79** AA/N Setchfield; **82** © Peter Barritt/Alamy; **82/83** © Danita Delimont/Alamy; **83** © Danita Delimont/Alamy; **84l** AA/N Setchfield; **84r** AA/N Setchfield; **84/85** AA/N Setchfield; **85t** AA/N Setchfield; **85c** AA/N Setchfield; **86l** AA/C Saywer; **86r** AA/N Setchfield; **87t** AA/N Setchfield; **87b** AA/N Setchfield; **88** AA/N Setchfield; **89** AA/N Setchfield; **90** AA/N Setchfield; **91** AA/N Setchfield; **92** AA/C Sawyer; **93** AA/C Sawyer; **96l** AA/N Setchfield; **96c** AA/N Setchfield; **96r** AA/N Setchfield; **97l** AA/C Sawyer; **97c** AA/C Sawyer; **97r** AA/N Setchfield; **98l** AA/N Setchfield; **98r** AA/N Setchfield; **98l** AA/N Setchfield; **99c** AA/N Setchfield; **99r** AA/N Setchfield; **100l** AA/N Setchfield; **100r** AA/N Setchfield; **101l** AA/C Sawyer; **101r** AA/C Sawyer; **102l** AA/N Setchfield; **102r** AA/N Setchfield; **103t** AA/N Setchfield; **103bl** AA/N Setchfield; **103br** AA/N Setchfield; **104** AA/N Setchfield; **105** AA/N Setchfield; **106** AA/C Sawyer; **107** © TTL Images/Alamy; **108t** AA/C Sawyer; **108tr** AA/N Setchfield; **108tcr** AA/N Setchfield; **108cr** AA/K Paterson; **108bcr** AA/A Mockford and N Bonetti; **108br** AA/N Setchfield; **109** AA/C Sawyer; **110** AA/C Sawyer; **111** AA/C Sawyer; **112** AA/C Sawyer; **113** AA/N Setchfield; **114** AA/N Setchfield; **115** AA/N Setchfield; **116** AA/N Setchfield; **117** AA/N Setchfield; **118** AA/N Setchfield; **119** AA/N Setchfield; **120t** AA/N Setchfield; **120l** European Central Bank; **121** AA/N Setchfield; **122** AA/N Setchfield; **123** AA/N Setchfield; **124t** AA/N Setchfield; **124bl** AA/N Setchfield; **124bcl** AA/N Setchfield; **124/125b** AA/N Setchfield; **125t** AA/N Setchfield; **125bc** AA/N Setchfield; **125bcr** AA; **125br** AA/N Setchfield